Congratulations for purchasing this book!

(Please fill in this form and post it at the given address)

Name : _____   _____
            (Surname)   (Name)

Date of Birth : _____   Profession : _____

Are you interested in going through the full course? Yes/No

Do you want the Certificates? Yes/No

Give names of your family members and their dates of birth:
(for absentee healing if the need arises these will be kept in
record with "THE HEALERS" group).

NAME   DATE OF BIRTH

_____   _____

_____   _____

_____   _____

_____   _____

_____   _____

_____   _____

You can always contact me at:

Mohan Makkar
C/o UBS Publishers' Distributors Ltd.
5 Ansari Road,
New Delhi-110 002 (India).

Mohan Makkar's

Reiki

Magic

(THE USUI SYSTEM)
&
Creative Visualisation Exercises

**THE SYMBOLS AND ATTUNEMENT TECHNIQUES
REVEALED STEP BY STEP
(Completely Illustrated)**

 UBSPD

UBS Publishers' Distributors Ltd.
New Delhi ● Bangalore ● Chennai
Calcutta ● Patna ● Kanpur ● London

UBS Publishers' Distributors Ltd.

5 Ansari Road, New Delhi-110 002
Phones : 3273601, 3266646 ● *Cable* : ALLBOOKS ● *Fax* : 3276593, 3274261
e-mail: ubspddel@del3.vsnl.net.in ● Internet: www.ubspd.com
10 First Main Road, Gandhi Nagar, Bangalore-560 009
Phones : 2263901, 2263902, 2253903 ● *Cable* : ALLBOOKS ● *Fax* : 2263904
6, Sivaganga Road, Nungambakkam, Chennai-600 034
Phones : 8276355, 8270189 ● *Cable* : UBSIPUB ● *Fax* : 8278920
8/1-B, Chowringhee Lane, Calcutta-700 016
Phones : 2441821, 2442910, 2449473 ● *Cable* : UBSIPUBS ● *Fax* : 2450027
e-mail: ubspdcal@cal.vsnl.net.in
5 A, Rajendra Nagar, Patna-800 016
Phones : 672856, 673973, 656170 ● *Cable* : UBSPUB ● *Fax* : 656169
80, Noronha Road, Cantonment, Kanpur-208 004
Phones : 369124, 362665, 357488 ● *Fax* : 315122

Distributors for Western India
M/s Preface Books
Shivali Apartments, Plot No. 1, S. No. 25/4, Chintamani Society,
Karve Nagar, Pune 411052 ● Phone: 346203

Overseas Contact
475 North Circular Road, Neasden, London NW2 7QG
Tele : 081-450-8667 ● *Fax* : 0181-452-6612 Attn: UBS

© Mohan Makkar

First Published **1999**
First Reprint **1999**

Cover Design: Ilaksha

Designed & Typeset at UBSPD in 11 pt New Times Roman ·
Printed at Nutech Photolithographers, Delhi (India).

My spiritual Guide
Satchitanand Satguru

Shri Sainath Maharaj of Shirdi
and
My Family — Neena, Nisha, Pooja,
Bharat and Prathna

DISCLAIMER

This book has been written by the author to provide information only. This book is not intended to replace professional medical care. If you believe that you may suffer from a physical or emotional impairment, seek care from a licensed health care professional. The information and exercises provided within this book are to be used at your own discretion. They are not offered in substitution for medical advice or treatment.

The author's goal is to complement medical care by encouraging healing of the body, mind and spirit. Best results are obtained by exercising common sense and body awareness in the practice of Reiki, Mind Control Techniques and Meditation and supplementing it with a healthy diet and lifestyle.

Acknowledgements

*M*y special thanks go first and foremost to Mrs. Manjusha and Pradeep Naik for introducing me to Reiki. I also thank and prostrate before my Reiki teacher, Dr. Pradeep Diwan, for imparting his knowledge with total devotion and dedication.

I thank all my 200-odd students for keeping in continuous contact with me and anxiously awaiting the publication of this book. I thank the 1400+ odd people treated and cured by our group "The Healers" who also await the release of this book.

I thank the members of our group "The Healers" now gaining wide recognition.

How can I forget Mr. Gautam and Mr. Ram of "Right Selection" bookshop for guiding me to the right direction that enabled the publication of this book?

Mrs. Fem Muralla and Mrs. Ganga Ramesh for editing this book. Specially the dedicated Mrs. Ganga Ramesh — I am at loss for words to describe her involvement with Reiki and her art of giving, giving and giving — *love*.

Ms. Vatsala — for a diamond was found by me, which the world threw away, thinking it was an ordinary glass. Vatsala has reached unattainable heights in such a short duration. She is a pride for any teacher.

My mother, who is also my first student, at the age of 75, is still spreading Reiki and having total faith in this unique art. My wife Neena, daughters Nisha, Pooja and Prathna, for being patient, understanding and full of love.

To all of you who are to become a part of our Reiki family.

Last but not the least — my voice within — my spiritual guides and my angels for giving me the strength and assurance that knowledge is like seeds, you have to sow to reap the harvest.

I have brought the light to you — may the darkness in your life vanish forever and may you live in everlasting happiness, peace and harmony.

Mohan Makkar

Contents

Part III
Reiki 2: Day 1

Part IV
Reiki 2: Day 2

Introduction

*W*elcome to Reiki Class 1. Let me introduce myself. I am your Reiki teacher. My name is Mohan. Before we proceed further I would like to tell you how I was introduced to *Reiki* — "*The Universal Healing Energy.*"

For the past few years I have been treating people by 'absentee healing' methods, an art that is hereditary and partially acquired through my father.

The main problem I faced while healing people was, unconsciously, I took the disease of the sick people upon myself. The results were always positive, people were healed, but I remained sick most of the time. So much so that my wife and children got tired of my sickness.

Pressure started building up. Finally, I got a notice from my wife — "I have had enough, either you choose treating the sick people or you choose me, I will not let you have both!" I was in a dilemma. I strongly believe that nature takes its own course, and in my case it did.

I met a girl named Manjusha. She contacted me for treating her mother who had 'frozen shoulders'. I treated her and Manjusha thanked me personally. At this time she declared that she was a Reiki master herself. What is *Reiki*? I asked her. She explained this to me.

I poured out my grievances to her. She suggested that I should go for a Reiki course. I did attend the Reiki course. Reiki 1 was through a teacher — who got me really fooled. I believe she is just a Reiki master and not a Reiki master/teacher. Attunements were given by the Reiki master and I believed that I had the power to heal without taking the illnesses on myself till the time I came across another Reiki master/teacher.

I went for a refresher course with the new Reiki master/ teacher and while doing the advance Reiki course (Reiki 2), he told me that my palms were not becoming warm as they should. This is the time when he asked me how the attunements were given. I explained to him, and he laughed. I knew that sarcastic laugh and understood that somewhere I had been cheated.

I paid the course fee of Reiki 1 and Reiki 2 to this Reiki master/teacher and started practising the new healing technique on my patients, physically and in absentia. At this juncture let me point out that I mixed my own techniques with the Reiki method and the results were superb.

I have treated cases like asthma, paralysis, arthritis, cough and colds, tooth aches, conjunctivitis, diabetes, rheumatism, spondilitis, migraine, memory lapses with astounding success. Presently, I am treating cases of blood plasma, diabetes, asthma, severed cornea, migraine, vertigo, lumbago, etc.

I have stopped remaining sick. The sicknesses of other people do not harm my health any more. I teach during the weekends and have witnessed the transformation of my students. I do not claim every student of mine has had a transformation. Actually, the results they get depend on the efforts they put in.

The more you practise, the more you gain. Nobody sees you, but remember you are your own judge and you will witness your own failings and your own successes. Be true and honest to yourself and you shall succeed. That is my promise.

During the complete course of Reiki — taking you gradually through to Reiki master/teacher's degree, we shall do some visual meditation exercises and learn the art of meditation also. We shall also touch on the topics of other healing techniques and discuss some of them.

For the visual meditation exercises, a technique of breathing will be taught to you, which you have to constantly practise and master.

Also, the secret symbols will be given to you and the art of attuning with easy-to-follow illustrations will be taught to you step by step.

A question may arise in your mind that there are dozens of books written on Reiki, so why another? Why this book? Without egoism I state that the idea of writing a unique book on Reiki was given to me and I thought of writing in a classroom format. How far I have succeeded in this effort is for you to decide.

This introduction can go on endlessly, but I will end here with a brief thought:

It is wisely said: You don't have to go to the sea and wait; to catch the fish, at least, you have to put the bait.

Like a well, the more Reiki energy you use, the more you will get — have happy Reiki-ing hours and wishing you perfect health.

Mohan Makkar

Part I

Reiki 1: Day 1

1

What Is Reiki?

*H*ave you read any book on Reiki?

There are many books available on this subject. The descriptions, the history, the principles are always the same. The story of Dr. Mikao Usui cannot be changed; neither can the characters of Dr. Hayashi or Mrs. Takata.

Reiki is made up of two syllables "REI" and "KI"?

"REI" stands for "UNIVERSAL" and "KI" stands for "ENERGY".

This explanation is best given in the book *Reiki* written by Bodo Baginski and Shalila Sharamon, which is as follows:

> This universal energy has existed amidst us from the beginning of the universe. Thousands of years ago the Tibetans already possessed a deep understanding of the nature of spirit, energy and matter. They used this knowledge to heal their bodies, harmonise their souls and lead their spirits to an experience of unity.
>
> This knowledge was guarded and preserved by the mystery schools and was available to a very few people, usually priests or spiritual leaders who in turn passed this technique to their disciples by word of mouth.
>
> The knowledge of Reiki would have remained lost forever had not Dr. Mikao Usui rediscovered the key which led to the recovery of a thousand-year-old tradition of healing in 2500-year-old Sanskrit sutras at the end of the nineteenth century.

Reiki — the universal energy — is defined as being that power which acts and lives in all created matter.

The Usui system of Reiki is not only the most simple and natural healing method we know of, but it is also the most effective way of transferring this universal life energy. Once the attunements are given to a person he becomes a Reiki channel and will remain so for the rest of his life.

We will mostly be talking about this universal life energy, which is the base of our classes — Reiki.

The human body consists of about 100 billion (100,000,000,000) cells. These cells in turn possess about 100,000 different genes, consisting of long, spiral-formed DNA chains. Every single one of these microscopically small cells contains within itself no less than the total genetic construction plans for our bodies.

If we were to roll out all these spiralled chains and join them up, their length would amount to more than 120 billion kilometres, about 800 times the distance between the earth and the sun. And yet all these chains of DNA molecules would fit into the size of a walnut.

Just think the greatness of the energy that all these forms of life manifest. How great must be the intelligence that gives these forms of life, shape and structure. The question that arises in our midst is: did our universe and our lives arise out of a chain of coincidences, as a materialistic view of things would have us believe? Can unconscious matter bring forth consciousness? Can it bring forth the spirit? The soul? Even scientists are baffled by these queries. The result is the same — that a superior intelligent force *does exist*. A universal spirit which is continually creating the universe out of itself.

Supergravitation theory describes the existence of a standardised, perfectly balanced field standing in relationship to only itself, a field of pure intelligence which brings forth all matter to form the basis of all creation. Wise men often tell the stories of a state of being containing all creation out of which all life arose. The energy of this state of being lives in all things, and it is this universal energy which flows through our hands in concentrated form when we treat someone with Reiki.

In short it means: Reiki has a holistic effect. It reaches all levels of existence and strives to bring these differing levels into a state of balance. The therapist is only a channel of energy, because it is not his own energy that passes through his hands, but it is a universal energy, which leaves the Reiki channel strengthened and harmonised. This universal energy seems to have a mind of its own, for it knows how much and where the person needs the energy. It is not for us to decide or in our control to add or subtract this energy.

Reiki is experienced as love. This love is a power, which unites us to a state of oneness with the whole of creation. Love is the original home of the soul.

Reiki is the healing method in the broadest sense of the word. For it not only heals the body, but the spiritual self also. Reiki has nothing to do with religion, spiritualism, occult in any shape or form. Neither is it a hypnotic nor any other psychological technique.

Today the rediscovery of Reiki has set forth a trend of healing techniques where no medicines are instilled in the body of the patient, no prayers are mumbled, yet the results are achieved. Reiki attunements bring forth the developments in you that have been dormant and you become a better person.

2

The History of Reiki

*T*he ancient healing method of Reiki was rediscovered in the middle of the nineteenth century by Dr. Mikao Usui, who was also responsible for its revival.

Grand Master Hawayo Takata (1900-1980) along the following lines has told the story of Dr. Usui's search for this secret knowledge:

Mikao Usui was the dean of a Christian college in Kyoto, Japan. One day, some of his pupils asked him why they had nothing of the healing methods used by Jesus Christ and whether Dr. Usui would be able to carry out such a healing for them. Since he was unable to answer these questions, Dr. Usui decided to resign from his position as per the Japanese customs.

He decided to study Christianity in a Christian country until he found the answers to the questions posed to him by his students.

His journey led him to America, where he attended the University of Chicago and became a Doctor of Theology. However, he could not find a satisfactory answer in Christian writings and, not having found one in Chinese scriptures either, he travelled to North India, where he was able to study the holy writings. Dr. Usui had not only the knowledge of Japanese, Chinese and English languages, but he also became a master of Sanskrit language.

He later returned to Japan where he discovered some Sanskrit formulas and symbols in old Buddhist sutras which seemed to hold the answers to his questions. At the time, he was living in a monastery in Kyoto, and, after he had spoken to the head, he set off to the Holy Mountain of Kuriyama, which lay 16 miles away. Here he intended to fast and meditate in solitude for 21 days in the hope of gaining contact with the level of consciousness. The Sanskrit symbols had been written in order to determine the truth of their contents.

Once he reached the top of the mountain, he laid 21 pebbles in front of him and removed one at the passing of each day as a kind of calendar. During this time, he read the sutras, sang and meditated. Nothing unusual happened until the last day dawned. It was still quite dark when he saw a small shining light moving towards him with great speed. He tried to get up and run, but as an after-thought he stayed put. The light became bigger and bigger and finally hit him in the middle of his forehead — the third eye chakra. Dr. Usui's thoughts were that he was going to die when he suddenly saw millions of little bubbles in blue, lilac, pink and all the colours of the rainbow. Then he saw a great white light, and the well-known Sanskrit symbols in front of him glowing in shining gold and he muttered "yes, I remember" before he fell unconscious. This was the birth of Reiki.

When Dr. Usui returned to the normal state of consciousness, the sun had already arisen. Though he had had a complete fast for 21 days, he was surprised to find that he felt full of strength and energy. He began to descend the mountain. In his rush, he stubbed his toe. Blood started flowing from the toe. Reflexively he covered the toe with the palm of his hand and much to his surprise the bleeding stopped and after a few moments the pain vanished. This was the first miracle.

Since he was hungry, he stopped at an inn and ordered a large Japanese breakfast. For those who do not know about Japanese breakfast, it can be stated that a single large Japanese breakfast can be easily shared with a friend or two with good appetites. The innkeeper saw Dr. Usui's clothes and his beard, and knew he had been fasting. He requested Dr. Usui to have soup and something light. But, Dr. Usui refused. He ate the complete Japanese breakfast without any side effects. This was the second miracle.

The innkeeper's granddaughter who served the food to him was suffering from a bad toothache. Her mouth was swollen. Dr. Usui asked the innkeeper if he could treat the child. The innkeeper somehow knew that his guest was no ordinary person. He gave Dr. Usui the permission. As soon as Dr. Usui laid his hands on the girl's cheeks, the pain vanished and after a few minutes the swelling also subsided. This was the third miracle.

Dr. Usui returned to the monastery, where his friend, the abbot, was lying in bed, suffering from arthritis. Dr. Usui sat beside him and placed his hands on the abbot. The abbot started feeling better and was mobile after a short period.

Dr. Usui decided to go to the Beggars City in the slums of Kyoto, treat the beggars and help them lead a better life. He spent seven years in the asylum, treating many diseases. One day, however, he saw the same faces. On querying why they kept coming back, he got the answer that begging was a better way of life than taking the burden of getting married and raising children and having a routine job.

Dr. Usui was deeply shaken and wept. He knew that he had forgotten something of great importance, namely, to teach the beggars gratitude. In the following days he thought out some Reiki maxims (see Chapter 5).

Soon afterwards Dr. Usui left the asylum and returned to Kyoto, where he kindled a large torch and stood in the streets. Asked for the reason by the passersby, Dr. Usui told them he was looking for people in search of the true light, people who were ill/oppressed and who were longing to be healed. This was the beginning of his new phase where he spent time travelling around and teaching Reiki.

Dr. Usui gave up his body and is now buried in a Kyoto temple, with the story of his life written on his gravestone. It is said that his grave was honoured by the Emperor of Japan.

One of Dr. Usui's closest collaborators, Dr. Chijiro Hayashi, took his place, becoming the second Reiki grand master in the line of tradition. He ran a private Reiki clinic in Tokyo until 1940, where unusually severe cases could be treated, with Reiki being applied "round the clock" specially in the event of serious illnesses. Frequently a patient would also receive Reiki from several practitioners at once. The effects of the Second World War and the death of Dr. Hayashi on 10 May, 1941 put an end to his work.

Mrs. Hawayo Takata became Dr. Hayashi's successor. She was born in 1900 on the island of Hawaii as a child of Japanese parents but was a citizen of the United States. She was a widow with two small children. She was suffering from a number of severe illnesses at the time when an inner voice told her to go to Japan and seek healing there.

Having arrived in Japan, she was lying on the operating table, about to undergo an operation, when the voice spoke to her again, telling her that the operation was unnecessary. She asked her doctor about other methods of treatment and he advised her to go to Dr. Hayashi's Reiki clinic. Once there, she was applied Reiki daily by two practitioners and, after a few months, she had won back her health completely.

Hawayo Takata became a pupil of Dr. Hayashi for a period of one year and then returned to Hawaii with her daughters. She was made a Reiki master by Dr. Hayashi when he visited Hawaii in 1938. On his death in 1941, she succeeded him as the grand master. She lived and healed in Hawaii for many years, but she first began to train Reiki masters herself when she was in her seventies. On 11 December 1980, Hawayo Takata passed away, leaving 22 Reiki grand masters in the USA and Canada.

Today there are 3500 to 4000 Reiki masters/teachers in the world. A book is being published by the Reiki Masters Group which gives the names and addresses of all the Reiki masters/ teachers in the world.

3

The Breathing Technique

Let's learn the breathing technique. This breathing exercise will help you to centralise your thoughts and keep your mind from wandering, whilst curing innumerable diseases like allergies, asthma, migraines, heart, lungs, stomach, liver problems etc.

Step 1: Take a deep breath in from your nose to your navel chord (belly button) to the count of 4. Inflate your stomach as much as possible while breathing in. Breathe in with me 1...2...3...4 - stop.

Step 2: Hold your breath to the count of 4: 1.... 2.... 3.... 4.

Step 3: Now breathe out slowly through your mouth, 1.... 2.... 3...4; deflate your stomach as you breathe out.

Step 4: Hold your breath to the count of 4.

Continue the same till you feel completely relaxed or slightly dizzy.

What happens is this:

From the time we are born to the time we depart this world we breathe. But, nobody teaches us how to breathe. What we do is we swim in the shallow waters, we never go into the deep. In between the thorax and trunk there are no bones. There are only floating ribs. These ribs survive on air. If we do not breathe in properly, we start to curl up. You may have seen cases of elderly people who curl up as age increases.

What we have to do is to breathe in deeply through the nose until we feel the air go to the navel. Hold the breath in there to the count of 4, and then release the breath through the mouth.

Twelve sets in the morning, 12 in the afternoon and 12 late evening will work wonders. For instance, those small ailments, like sinus, coughs and cold, memory lapses, headaches, migraines, body aches, allergies, asthmatic attacks, will be cured. You will feel the difference yourself. So, why not start now?

(Care has to be taken not to overdo any of the exercises, that are being taught to you. A correct dose of anything will help you maintain your health, but an overdose of anything can ruin your health. So, please take care to do and follow what is being specified.)

Note: **Not recommended for patients with heart problems.**

4

A Visual Meditation Exercise:
The White Light Meditation

*I*n every Reiki class, we do a meditation known as the "White Light Meditation". During this meditation, we heal the world by sending a flow of positive energy to make our world a better place to live in.

- Do your breathing exercise as taught to you. (4 breathes in, 4 hold, 4 out and 4 hold — repeat) — only 3 or maximum 4 sets. We will call this CENTRALISING for future records.
- Now, on an out breath, with your mental power create a white ball, the size of a tennis ball. Make this ball spin with your mental power of visualisation. Visualise it, see it with your mental eyes in front of your third eye chakra, the centre of your eyebrows. See it spin, slow.... slow.... slow, now it is picking up speed fast...fast.... faster...faster.
- As the speed is increasing, visualise a white light emitting from the ball, this white light is like a mist, a fog. See the white light cover the ball. The amazing thing you notice is that this white light is floating and covering you and the furniture in the room. See the hazy mist cover the room.
- Let this light float into the other rooms, the kitchen, the bathroom, the storeroom, the bedroom and all the other rooms in your apartment. Now, extend your vision, see it seep out of the balcony doors, the windows, the main door and visualise it going out into the street. Visualise the white light covering your building.

12

- The speed of the white light is increasing. The white light is now covering the area in which you live. See the white light cover the town and the city you live in.
- See the white light cover the other surrounding cities.
- See the white light cover the entire nation. The white light is now covering surrounding nations and the full world.
- Visualise the white light cover all the mentally handicapped children. See the children improving under the influence of this white light. See them becoming better and better and better. See the white light cover all the pregnant women. Visualise the pregnant women delivering healthy children normally. Visualise the white light cover the people with terminal diseases like cancer and AIDS. See these people recovering. Visualise the white light cover all the undernourished children on this planet. Visualise these children eating lavishly. See them recovering gradually and learning to smile. Visualise the white light cover all the prisons in this world. Visualise the prisoners turn into better humans.
- Visualise the world leaders signing a peace treaty under the white light.
- Visualise the terrorists throw up their arms and surrender.
- Visualise brotherhood and love floating in every heart in every being. Visualise all politicians turning to new leaves and working for the benefit of mankind. Keep this visualisation in the level of your third eye chakra.

Slowly come back to the room and open your eyes whenever you feel like it.

At this time I will take a short break.

Why don't you also relax for five minutes? Have a nice cup of hot tea/coffee or sip a cold juice.

5

The Five Principles of Reiki

*D*r. Usui was deeply shaken on finding the beggars returning to the beggar city. He knew that he had forgotten to teach them gratitude. So he thought of the following maxims, which are today known as "THE FIVE PRINCIPLES OF REIKI"

(1) *JUST FOR TODAY, I WILL LIVE BY THE ATTITUDE OF GRATITUDE.*
(2) *JUST FOR TODAY, I WILL NOT WORRY.*
(3) *JUST FOR TODAY, I WILL NOT GET ANGRY..*
(4) *JUST FOR TODAY, I WILL EARN MY LIVING HONESTLY.*
(5) *JUST FOR TODAY, I WILL HONOUR MY PARENTS, TEACHERS AND ELDERS.*

1. JUST FOR TODAY, I WILL LIVE BY THE ATTITUDE OF GRATITUDE

To live in gratitude is to live in abundance. When we are constantly in the attitude of gratitude, feeling thankful not only for what we have received but for what we know and trust will constantly be provided, we begin to magnetically attract abundance. Our normal state is that of abundance. It is only our connection with the race mind consciousness (or collective unconscious) or lack of it and our own conditioning, which keeps us from accepting that which is truly ours. One of the fundamental concepts at the root of the major philosophical and religious systems in ancient times was that of all-sufficiency. It was taught that to understand one's self was to understand God, that by going deep within, one could transmute fear into love, ignorance into wisdom, and lack into abundance.

Jesus said: "...What you see you shall be." In other words, if you focus on what you do not have, you will continue to be in lack. On the other hand, if you continue to be aware of the unlimited abundance all around you, and constantly feel the resulting gratitude, abundance will continue to be your state of affairs, and even increase. There is nothing lacking on this planet, it is the distribution system that has gone haywire due to our illusions about lack, not to mention man's greed, due again, to fear of lack, that has indeed kept us in the very state we fear.

To be in gratitude is to know at the core of your being that all is one, that separation is an illusion. Another important factor is to be able to accept the abundance that is rightfully ours. If we feel subconsciously "unworthy" of the riches and wealth of the universe, we will block the flow of abundance to us. Many people now suffer from this consciousness of separation from the absolute — which embodies all that is. The long history of guilt of separation from the absolute keep even those people who seem to follow and live in accord with the laws of universal harmony, away from the true success and prosperity which is rightfully theirs. The causal factor must be sought in each individual.

In most cases, the channels through which affluence and harmony normally flow are either under developed or paralysed. Universal life energy must then be used in order to give to those channels their natural functions. Once this connection is made, success and prosperity will be obtained. In the realm of the absolute, every action, every cause, results in a perfect effect, which is complete success. The only reason that most people do not achieve it is because they are not aligned with it, or are closed to it.

2. JUST FOR TODAY, I WILL NOT WORRY

To worry is to forget that there is a divine or universal purpose to everything. If we are truly in tune with the guidance of our higher-selves, and live each day to the best of our ability, we are then aware that we have done everything in our power that we possibly can, and the rest is up to the universal life force. Worry is a thought pattern, which results from a feeling of separateness from the "Universal Life Force" consciousness. To worry about the past is futile — we must remember that each person, including ourselves, does the best that he can in each of life's situations, in accordance with the knowledge or wish he has at any given moment. We are all products of our conditioning and tend to reach accordingly. If we regret a past action of ours, realise that we reacted according to our resources; then we should be thankful for the lesson and move on. At the same time, realise that all injustices done to us in the past were done by others as a result of their conditioning. We can only wish them well and hope that they too have learned from their actions.

To worry about the future is also futile. It is said: "Expect the best in life, and, when you receive something that you didn't expect, acknowledge that it is the best for you in your present situation." Even if what occurs seems very negative at the time, it is only a lesson. Somehow, we helped create that situation, even if on a subconscious level, to learn. So feel gratitude that it has come to pass, and that we are free; then move on. Surrender, to the higher self, and try not to interfere with the universal timing in life. Know that in our perfect flow there is a synchronicity of events, as long as we have completed our part in the scheme of things, all else will be taken care of. Worrying results from illogical and irrational patterns of thought, creating in turn more limitations and a further separation in consciousness. We should surrender today to our higher self's plan and release ourselves from worry.

3. JUST FOR TODAY, I WILL NOT GET ANGRY

Anger, in reality, is a totally unnecessary emotion. Like most inappropriate reactive emotions, it has its roots in the feeling of guilt from having separated ourselves from the universal consciousness. To anger is to desire no control, which results from feeling out of control, indeed out of synchronisation with our divine or universal life purpose. Many people allowed their ego to direct their life course, at the same time ignoring the inner guidance, which would otherwise lead them to a natural and harmonious flow. By allowing the ego to be affected by inappropriate desires and expectations, we suffer untold grief.

When our expectations get the best of us, and we become angry, because someone didn't live up to our needs and desires, we tend to forget that those we have drawn into our environment are only our mirrors. Every thought that we think sets up a cause, and the effect may come back when we least expect it. Truly, every situation is a mirror, a direct reflection of cause and effect, created by us. Those who happen to "press our buttons" or stimulate our weak points are not really the causes of our anger. They are there to learn as well. We drew each other in a mutual need to complete certain lessons. When someone spurs us on to anger, we should try to stop the emotion (refer the art of living) by observing our reactions to others and ourselves and become more consciously aware of our reactions, and, in time, master our emotions. We should also feel gratitude for having been given the opportunity to witness our weak points, as only growth can result.

Ultimately, if we do get angry, we should not feel guilty for experiencing that anger. It has been programmed into us for so many generations that it is difficult at first not to be triggered when we are "attacked" by the anger of others. In addition, we have long allowed our expectations to get the best of us, and tend to take things personally when things don't go our way.

The hurt feelings, which result, cause us to blast out in anger. While attempting to "reprogramme our old anger tapes", we must allow ourselves to release our emotions, and not hold anger in. What we can do is tone down our reactions by expressing, in a calm way, how someone's negative statement makes us feel. If the other person persists in a loud way, it is wise to leave their vicinity and regain our power by not reacting. The best action to take, in the beginning of any episode, is not to react, but to emanate love. It is difficult to feel anger while we are smiling. Our smile may even trigger a "mirror effect" in the other person.

Finally, anger is a very disharmonious energy, which creates disease in the body. It would be of great benefit to learn to transform this energy by dealing with it constructively. Just for today do not anger — be in attitude of gratitude.

4. JUST FOR TODAY I WILL EARN MY LIVING HONESTLY

Of great importance to a harmonious life flow is honesty in dealing with oneself. To be honest with oneself is to face the truth in all things. Many of us live in a fantasy world when it comes to perceiving reality. When we deny the truth about reality and are ultimately faced with truth, we may become severely disjointed. Sometimes the truth seems hard to deal with in our world, but if we look deeply, examine our own behaviour, and discover the purposes that various people and situations have in our lives, we will develop compassion for all.

To live in trust is to be aligned with our higher self's purpose. Living in truth is also the simplest, least complex way to live. Truth brings clarity. When we face life honestly, we can see more clearly the lessons we are here to learn, and complete them with much less effort. Living a life of illusion is much more complex. Denial then takes a centre focus, and soon a web of falsehoods may so thoroughly bind us to "protect" us from the truth that we may have difficulty finding our way out of the maze.

If we are honest with ourselves, we will tend to project honesty onto others. It then becomes easy to "do unto others as you would have others do unto you". When we do our work honestly, we are being truthful to our higher self. This truth is reinforced by love for others, and ourselves, which helps to create harmony in our life. So, let's live in truth vitalised by love, and just for today do our work honestly.

5. JUST FOR TODAY, I WILL HONOUR MY PARENTS, TEACHERS AND ELDERS

Truly, we are all of one source. It is also clear that all forms of life are interdependent. The destructive changes that have occurred in recent times on the planet (which have happened as a result of man's insensitivity to the delicate ecological balance) have opened us up to this fact. In order to survive, we are discovering that we will have to drop our self-centered tendency to want to control nature, and learn to show love and respect for all life forms.

Through the study of physics, we now know that we are all a collective energy from the same source. There is truly no solid matter, only different levels of vibrations. All forms of matter vibrate at different energy levels, yet they are all interconnected, because there are not solid barriers between them. Thus when we accept all of the various aspects of ourselves, it affects all others. Likewise, when we accept others, we too feel the reflection in ourselves. As a result, any positive energy, whether directed at ourselves or others, helps to heal the whole planet. Each person, animal, plant and mineral is included in the whole. To show love and respect to all others is to love and respect ourselves and our mother earth, so, just for today, show love and respect for every living being.

6

The Art of Living*

*E*veryone seeks peace and harmony because these are what we lack in our lives. From time to time we all experience agitation, irritation, disharmony and suffering. When one suffers from agitation, one does not keep this misery limited to oneself but, instead, one keeps distributing it to others. The agitation permeates into the atmosphere around the miserable person. Everyone else, who comes into contact with him/her, becomes irritated and agitated. Certainly this is not the right way to live.

One ought to be at peace within oneself and at peace with all others. After all, a human being is a social being. He has to live in a society and deal with others. How can he live peacefully? How can we maintain harmony within ourselves, and around us, so that others also can live peacefully?

When one is agitated, one has to know the basic reason for the agitation, the cause of the suffering. If one investigates the problem, it soon becomes clear that whenever one starts generating any negativity or defilement in the mind, one becomes agitated. A negativity in the mind, a mental defilement or impurity cannot co-exist with peace and harmony.

How does one start generating negativity? You become very unhappy when you find someone behaving in a way which you don't like. Unwanted events take place and create tensions within me. Desired events do not take place, some obstacles come in the way, and again create tensions within me, I start tying knots within

---

* A discourse by D. N. Goenka — Vipasna Meditation

myself. And throughout life, unwanted things keep on happening, desired things may or may not take place, and this process of reaction, of tying knots, makes the entire mental and physical structure so tense, so full of negativity that life becomes miserable.

Now, one way to solve the problem is to arrange things in such a way that nothing unwanted happens in your life, and that everything keeps on happening exactly as you wish to. You must develop such a power, or somebody else must have the power and must come to your aid when you request him that nothing unwanted happens in your life, and that everything you want should keep on happening. But this is not possible. There is no one in the world, whose desires are always fulfilled, in whose life everything happens according to his wishes, without anything undesirable happening. Things continue to occur contrary to our desires and wishes. Then, in spite of these undesirable events, how can we react sensibly? How to avoid tension? How to remain peaceful and harmonious?

Wise and saintly persons in India and many other countries studied this problem of human suffering and gave a solution. If something unwanted happens and one starts to react by generating anger, fear or any negativity, then as soon as possible, one should divert one's attention to something else. Divert your mind. Get up, take a glass of water, and start drinking. Your anger will not multiply, you will rule anger. Or start counting, 1,2,3,4,5… etc. Else, start repeating a word, phrase, and any God's name, *mantra* just to divert your mind and come out of the negativity, out of the anger.

This solution was indeed helpful. It worked. It still works. When you are angry dig a hole and plant a tree. Or bury yourself in the pages of an interesting book, put on some music and dance, work out in a gym or practise boxing. Personally stonewash your jeans. Write out the reason for your anger and shred the paper to bits and when you throw the paper, throw your anger away also. Practise playing some percussion instruments, the drums, tabla, anything. Channelise that angry energy in some creative manner. Practising this, the mind feels free from agitation.

In fact, the solution works only at the conscious level. Actually, by diverting the attention, one pushes the negativity deep into the unconscious, and on this level one continues to generate and multiply the same defilement. At the surface level there is a layer of peace and harmony, but in the depths of the mind is a sleeping volcano of suppressed negativity which sooner or later will erupt violently.

Other explorers of the inner truth went still further in their search; and by experiencing the reality of mind and matter within themselves, they recognised that diverting the attention is only running away from the problems. Escape is not the solution; one must face the problem. Whenever negativity arises in the mind, just observe it, face it. As soon as one starts observing any mental defilement, then it begins to lose all its strength. Slowly it withers away and is uprooted.

A good solution, avoiding both the extremes of suppression and free licence, keeping the negativity in the unconscious will not eradicate it; and allowing it to manifest in the physical or vocal action will only create more problems. But, if one just observes, then the defilement passes away, and one has eradicated that negativity and is freed from the defilement.

This sounds wonderful, but is it really practicable? For an average person, is it easy to face the defilement? When anger rises, it overpowers us so quickly that we don't even notice it. Then, overpowered by anger, we commit certain actions physically or vocally which are harmful to us and to others. Later, when the anger has passed, we cry and ask for forgiveness, only to repeat the actions in the future.

The difficulty is that I am not aware when defilement sets in. It begins deep at the unconscious level of the mind; and by the time it reaches the conscious level, it gains so much strength that it overwhelms me and I cannot observe it.

Then, I must keep a private secretary to remind me so that whenever the anger sets in, he says, "Look, you are getting angry". And since I do not know the time when anger will set in, I should keep three secretaries at three eight-hour shifts.

Moreover, when my secretary reminds me that the anger is setting in, I will slap him and ask him. "Do you think you are paid to teach me?" I am so overpowered by anger that no good advice will help.

Even though I act like a thorough gentleman, I will tell him that I will now watch my anger. When I close your eyes, the cause of the anger will be playing in my mind, the incident which has made me angry will be replayed. This means I am not observing the anger, I am stimulating my emotions and myself. This will act as oil to fire, and will multiply the anger. It is indeed very difficult to observe any abstract negativity, abstract emotion, divorced from the external object, which arouses it.

But, one who has reached the ultimate truth has found a real solution. He has discovered that whenever any defilement arises in the mind, simultaneously two things happen at the physical level. The breath loses it normal rhythm. You start breathing hard whenever any negativity comes into the mind. This is one reality, which everyone can experience though it is very gross and apparent. And at a subtler level, some kind of biochemical reaction starts within the body, some sensation. Defilement will generate a sensation of one kind or another in some part of the body.

This is a practical solution. An ordinary person cannot observe abstract defilements of the mind, abstract fear, anger or passion. But with proper training and practice, it is very easy to observe the respiration and the sensations, slow down the fast-paced breathing and calm the sensations, both of which are related to the mental defilement.

The respiration and sensations will help me in two ways. Firstly, they will be your private secretaries. As soon as defilement starts in the mind, your breath will lose its rhythm, its normality, and it will start shouting, "Look, something has gone wrong!" You cannot slap the breath. You have to accept the warning. Secondly, the sensations tell me, "Something has gone wrong", you must accept it. Then, having been warned, you start observing the respiration, the sensations, and you find very quickly that the defilement passes away.

This mental-physical phenomenon is like a coin with two sides. On one side is whatever thoughts or emotions arising in the mind. On the other side are the respiration and sensation in the body. Any thought or emotion, whether conscious or unconscious, any mental defilement manifests in the breath and sensations of the moment. Thus, by observing the respiration or the sensation, you are indirectly observing the mental defilement. Instead of running away from the problem, you are facing the reality as it is. Then you shall find that the defilement loses its strength. It can no longer overpower as it did in the past. If you persist, the defilement eventually disappears altogether; and you remain peaceful and happy.

In this way, the technique of self-observation shows us reality in its two aspects — inner and outer. Previously, one always looked with open eyes, missing the inner truth. You always looked outside for the cause of your unhappiness; you always blamed and tried to change the reality outside. Being ignorant of the inner reality, you never understood that the cause of suffering lies within your own blind reactions.

Now, by training, you can see the other side of the coin. You are aware of what is happening inside you. And whatever it is, whatever sensation, you learn just to observe it without losing the balance of mind. You stop reacting, stop multiplying your miseries. Instead, you now allow the defilement to manifest and pass away.

Gradually, after constant practice, you find that you are free from your negativities and defilements. You are becoming purer and purer. Your mind is being filled with love, unassuming love for others, full of compassion for the failings and sufferings of others; full of joy at their success and happiness, full of equanimity in the face of any situation.

I also know the truth that your balanced mind has not only become peaceful in itself, but is helping others also to become peaceful. The atmosphere surrounding you makes others peaceful too.

In such an atmosphere one can be more effective in society. While in anger there is only destruction, in peace and equanimity there can be constructive and effective changes to society.

7

The Reiki Alliance

*J*ust before the demise of Grand Master Mrs. Hawayo Takata on 11 December, 1980, Mrs. Takata and some of the Reiki masters founded in August, 1980 the American Reiki Association which was to organise and co-ordinate the passing on of the knowledge of Reiki:

Today, Reiki is represented by two organisations which have succeeded the first and which are both based in the USA. One has been the American International Reiki Association Inc. (The AIRA now called the TR̈TAI) and the other is the Reiki Alliance.

The Reiki Alliance was founded in 1981 by Phyllis Lee Furumoto, the grand-daughter of Mrs. Hawayo Takata, and a group of 22 Reiki masters, in the form of an open association. The Reiki Alliance was registered in the USA as a non-profit organisation in 1981, with Phyllis Lee Furumoto holding the position of the grand master. At the beginning of 1987, about 100 Reiki masters, some living in Europe, were members of the Alliance. Most of the masters trained by Hawayo Takata belong to this organisation. The Reiki Alliance takes a spiritual approach to the spreading of Reiki and keeps to the traditional teachings. The Alliance is of the opinion that the truth finds its way to the hearts of those open and prepared for it and, therefore, they rarely advertise.

The American International Reiki Association Inc. was founded in 1982 by Dr. Barbara Weber Ray. Dr. Ray had also been trained by Hawayo Takata to convey the knowledge involved in the attainment of the master grade to others and became the president of this group. The AIRA has been concerned with research into scientific aspects of Reiki to a large extent and is known for its well-organised publicity efforts. It has founded a Reiki documentation centre and carries out symposiums, conferences and exhibitions and is active in public events. The association also trains teachers of Reiki.

We are of the opinion that both complement each other in their efforts to teach and spread the idea of Reiki. If a feeling arises that you should join one of them, search your heart, rely on your intuition and join the organisation that best answers your needs.

8

Visual Meditation: The Lily Pond

- Relax.
- Do the centralising exercise.
- Good.
- Now close your eyes.
- Relax.
- No thoughts are coming to you. You are totally comfortable and relaxed. Relax...Relax.... Relax.
- Visualise yourself outside a building, which looks exactly like the white house. See yourself outside this building. You can see a sign on the top of the building, which reads *THE LILY POND*.
- You make an immediate decision to visit the lily pond.
- You start climbing the steps. 1.... 2.... 3...4...5...6...7...8...9.... 10. Now, you are in front of the main door. Visualise yourself raising your hand and pushing the door inwards. Now, you are stepping into the Lily Pond.
- You are in the main hall where the lily pond is.
- What you see now before you are a number of steps which are going downwards.
- At the bottom it is semi-darkness. You are feeling relaxed. A certain peace, calm is touching you and for some unknown reasons you are feeling internally happy, you are feeling happy.... happy...very happy.
- You start descending the steps. One, go slow, go with peace, for this is a magical world. Step 2, now slowly, Step 3.

- As you set your foot on step 3, suddenly dim lights are turned on. You continue descending, step 4, now you can hear a soft music in the background.
- Step 5; the hall is lit up, everything is clear. Visualise a big lily in front of you, in the centre of a pond. See its colours and the strong green petals, surrounded by the background of the sky with its red, orange, blue, violet, indigo colours because of the rising sun. See the rainbow beyond the lily. Look at the serene atmosphere in and above the hall.
- See yourself taking off your clothes and stepping into the pond. Swim if you may. Talk to the fish, ride on the back of the big tortoise in the pond.
- If you wish to fly towards the sky, do so. Relax. You are free of worries. Now, visualise coming downwards and resting in the centre of the Lily. Relax. Relax.
- Take a deep breath. Relax. Visualise yourself in the pond swimming lazily, take a dip into the water. See yourself coming out of the water. Look around you, what you see is the water turning blackish in colour. See the water turn back to its natural colour. Take a dip again. Again you see the blackened water surrounding you. This blackness is the negativity inside you, which is coming out of your system. Continue taking dips till you see that the water is clear.
- Visualise yourself coming out of the lily pond. Wear your clothes. You need not dry yourself. As you can see your body has already dried as you stepped out of the lily pond.
- Leave the building.
- Relax — try to feel the sensations in your body.
- Open your eyes whenever you feel like it.

Note: Most of the students who have done this exercise in my classroom have had different experiences. Some of them feel giddy, some of them feel elated, and some feel completely positive.

This is a Silva Mind Control Exercise.

9

Chakras

*C*hakras are the psychic centres in the body that are active at all times, whether we are conscious of them or not. Energy moves through the chakras to produce different psychic states. Modern biological science explains this as the chemical changes produced by the endocrine glands, ductless glands whose secretions mix into the body's bloodstream directly and instantaneously.

Ancient philosophers of the East related those changes with the five basic elements viz., earth, water, fire, air and ether.

Knowledge about the chakras can be a valuable key to introspection. It is possible to observe oneself and see energy moving through the various psychic centres. Religious practices such as fasting, charity and selfless service cause the energy to flow into the higher centres; the dormant energy coiled in the "root chakra" becomes active — and begins its ascent. After the flow has reached the higher centres, the total attitude of the practitioner changes; this feeling is referred to repeatedly as a new birth.

Maintaining the upward flow of energy then becomes the primary concern of such a person. The constant, simultaneous practice of visualisation and recitation of mantras help the aspirant to maintain the flow of energy in higher centres — and thus get beyond the elements.

Chakras are basics to the awakening of the Kundalini. But, in Reiki, the sole purpose of studying the chakras is to give more energy to these chakras to help activate our body more healthily.

In the Kundalini tradition, there are seven distinct energy centres known to exist in the human body, located up and down the spine and also in the brain itself. In a more contemporary scientific understanding, the inner energy vortexes empowering the human organism are understood in terms of the electromagnetic dynamics of subatomic physics. The chakras are in fact a primal expression of the cosmic dance described by subatomic physicists as a spontaneous shifting of matter into energy, energy into matter, and matter back into energy again.

As Einstein clearly posited — and ancient yogic masters knew many thousands of years before — our bodies are not just material in nature. They are also quite definitely energetic in nature. Science has amassed considerable knowledge concerning this electromagnetic, bioenergetic functioning of the human body. But scientists are first to admit that they don't really comprehend the underlying forces that generate life. Scientific instruments can look only so far into the matter-energy continuum, before reaching their perceptual limits.

We give below the names, positions and colours of the Chakras:

NAMES OF CHAKRAS	POSITIONS	COLOURS
CROWN	2" TO 3" ABOVE HEAD	VIOLET
3RD EYE	CENTRE OF EYEBROWS	INDIGO-DARK BLUE
THROAT	THROAT	LIGHT SHINY BLUE
HEART	CENTRE OF BREASTS	DARK GREEN
SOLAR PLEXUS	SOLAR PLEXUS/NAVAL REGION	SHINY YELLOW
SEXUAL	THE GENITAL REGION	SHINY ORANGE
ROOT	BASE OF SPINE	DARK RED

What do these Chakras represent?

The Root Chakra: The Root Chakra is the first chakra and is most powerfully related to our contact with the earth, our home planet. The physical nerve bundle at the base of the spine that is associated with the root chakra does look like a massive root system that leaves our spine and runs down both legs like a massive root system down both legs as the sciatic nerve. This is the largest peripheral nerve system in our body. It is as thick as our thumb as it leaves the sacral plexus at the base of our pelvis and spreads like a great root system down each leg, all the way to the tips of our toes and the bottoms of our heels. Some people consider this root chakra a lowly, unimportant energy centre. Others, especially in recent years, revere it with utmost respect. So, the root chakra, which provides us without connection to mother earth at a most primal level, should be held as equal to the crown chakra at the top of the head.

The Sexual Chakra: The key function of the sexual chakra is to manifest primal creative energy into the form of functional sexual energy — which the nervous system can then transmute into higher vibrations of spiritual energy.

The Solar Plexus/Navel Chakra: This chakra is a beautifully complex energy centre; it deals with personal power, organisational capacity, and the ability to go into action to manifest our ideas in the physical world. This chakra is also linked with the tendency to employ occult powers to manipulate the environment and fellow human beings. In a more positive light, this chakra's power is used to initiate contact with the spiritual dimensions of life that become more fully developed as we awaken the higher chakras.

The Heart Chakra: The heart chakra is associated with a magical quality — a quality we call *love*, which ideally serves as the underpinning of all the other chakra qualities of the human energetic system. The heart chakra, in its most basic sense, is the marriage of matter and spirit, of concrete and abstract, of knowledge and wisdom, of earth and heaven. It lies at the centre, and when balanced with energies from above and below, serves as the true location of the creative force of the universe in the human body.

The Throat Chakra: The throat chakra is the chakra of interpersonal communication. Without it there would be no interchange of ideas from one person to another, and virtually no human civilisation at all. It makes perfect sense for the communication chakra to be in the throat region of the body, since there is where our basic communication tool is located — the larynx. Through this remarkable organ we are able to take the outflow of air through our windpipe, and, transform the rushing air into a vibratory message for the outside world to pick up and respond to.

The Third Eye Chakra: The first five chakras have been located down below the mind itself. Now, with the sixth chakra, we reach the point where we are consciously focusing on the part of our body that in fact is doing the conscious focusing: the mind is finally looking directly at itself. Whereas the fifth chakra was the chakra of sound, of relatively slow vibrations passing through the medium of air molecules in our planetary atmosphere, the sixth chakra is the chakra of light, of vibratory energy travelling remarkably fast, not needing an atmospheric medium for its transmission.

The Crown Chakra: The crown chakra is the swirling energy vortex located right in the top of our head and swirling also above the top of our head, where we transcend individual consciousness and tap into infinite consciousness. We cease to exist as a separate entity when we are in the seventh-chakra consciousness. The "Me" evaporates. There is only infinite consciousness, of which we are an integral part.

10

Self-Healing Technique: The Hand Positions

A fter the Reiki master/teacher gives the attunements to you, you will feel the warmth of your palms increases.

In a moment we will learn the hand positions and you have just to follow the instructions. After memorising the hand positions, you will have to give Reiki to yourself as illustrated in the next few pages:

The hand positions for the front side of the body is as follows:

1. Eyes — both palms covering both eyes.
2. Temples — both palms covering both temples.
3. Ears — both palms covering both temples.
4. Forehead and back of the head — any way you feel comfortable — one hand on forehead and the other on back of the head.
5. Both hands at the back of the head — one hand over the other — then at the back of the head.
6. Throat chakra — one hand on Adam's apple and the other at the back of your neck.
7. Thymus and thyroid glands — both hands just an inch and a half away from the Adam's apple.
8. Heart chakra — both hands in the centre of your breasts.
9. Solar plexus — both hands on point between the thorax and the navel cord.

10. Liver — both hands on liver — righthand side near to the solar plexus.
11. Lung tips — both hands on both the lung tips.
12. Pancreas/spleen — both hands on pancreas/spleen (opposite side of the lever — Lefthand side near to the solar plexus).
13. Hara — (4 fingers below the navel cord) — both hands on hara.
14. (a) Ovaries (ladies).
14. (b) Spermatic cords (men).
15. Thighs (left) and right.
16. Knees (left and right).
17. Calf-muscles (left and right).
18. Ankles and sole of foot (left).
19. Ankles and sole of foot (right).

REIKI POSITIONS FOR
FRONT SIDE OF THE BODY

Eyes   Fig - 1   Temples   Fig - 2

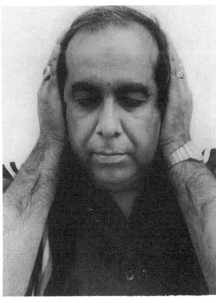 

Ears   Fig - 3   Front & Back of Head   Fig - 4

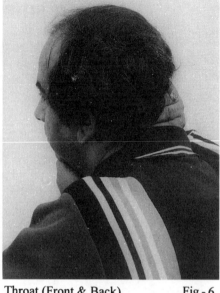

Back of Head   Fig - 5   Throat (Front & Back)   Fig - 6

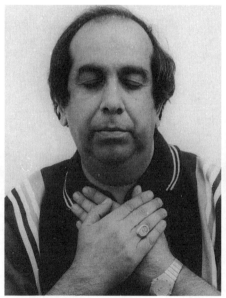

Thymus & Thyroid Glands   Fig - 7   Heart   Fig - 8

Solar Plexus   Fig - 9

Liver   Fig - 10

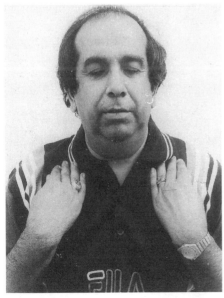

Shoulder Tips   Fig - 11

Pancreas & Spleen   Fig - 12

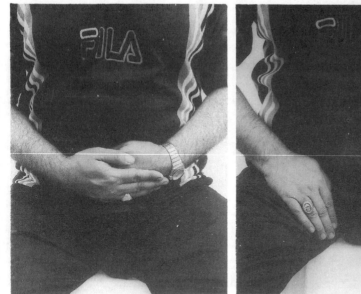

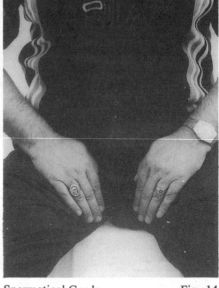

Hara   Fig - 13   Spermatical Cords   Fig - 14

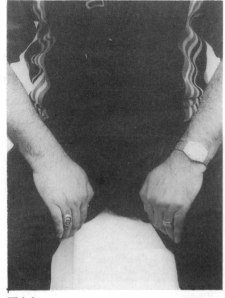

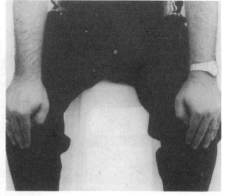

Thighs   Fig - 15   Knees   Fig - 16

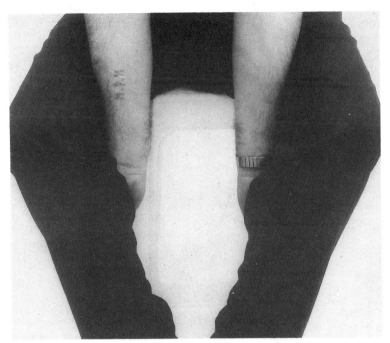

Calves   Fig - 17

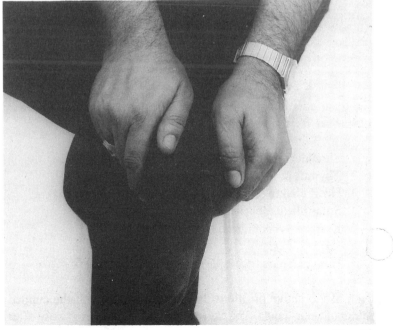

Left Foot   Fig - 18

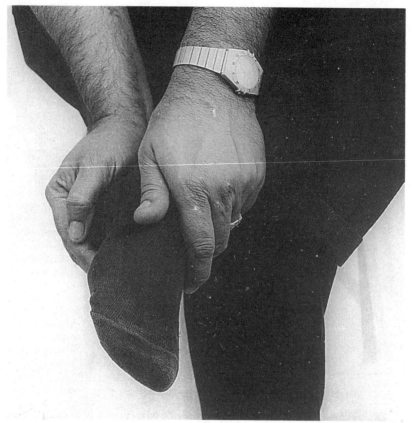

Right Foot   Fig - 19

The hand positions for the backside of the body are as follows:
(please see photographs)

1. Shoulders (backside) — both hands on shoulders.
2. Thymus & thyroid glands (backside).
3. Heart chakra (backside) — both hands on heart chakra.
4. Solar plexus (backside).
5. Kidneys — both hands on both kidneys.
6. Hara (backside).
7. Base of Spine (backside) — this is Root Chakra

Each of the above position/s has to be covered with the cupped
palms of your hands. The Self-treatment is completed only after
the Balancing of the Chakras is done.

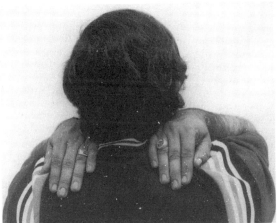

Shoulder Blades

Fig - 1

Thymus & Thyroid

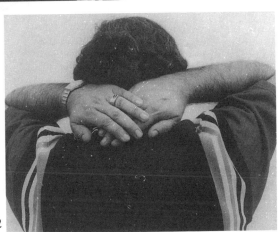

Fig - 2

Heart

Fig - 3

Solar Plexus   Fig - 4

Kidneys   Fig - 5

Hara   Fig - 6

Root Chakra/   Fig - 7
Base of Spine

11

Dos and Don'ts about Reiki

Dos

- Wash hands before and after giving Reiki — to stop the flow of energy.
- Have a conversation with the patient, ask him/her why the healing is required.
- Convince him/her to come for at least three to four days.
- Patient should wear loose clothing, empty his/her pockets, remove their rings and watches, belts and all/any metals.

Dont's

- Reiki patients should not cross their legs while taking Reiki energy.
- Every point covered must be for a minimum of three minutes — though the Reiki channel may or may not feel the energy passing through the palms.
- Do not make any diagnosis.

Pointers

- **Day 1:** The patient may be withdrawn, not knowing where the hands will be moving.
- **Day 2:** He/she will accept the movements of the hands and probably fall asleep as relaxed.
- **Day 3:** He/she may wait for some experience.
- **Day 4:** Will experience Reiki energy.

Please Take Care to

- keep a jug or glass of drinking water handy
- keep tissue paper handy
- explain to the patient that we are just Reiki Channels and the patient will be drawing as much energy as it required by his body
- always start Reiki with the head position
- Spirals. From right shoulder to right hand. Left shoulder to left hand. Right shoulder to right feet. Left shoulder to left feet.
- Chakra balancing on the back
- Stroking from top of spine to hara (back side)
- Caressing, also known as evening of Auras.

12

What if You Come Across Cold Areas?

*W*hen you become a Reiki channel and start using Reiki to treat your friends and relatives, you will notice at times that some of the parts where Reiki is being given are cold. (i.e., you will not feel any warmth in your palms nor will you feel that the patient is absorbing any energy). So what do you do?

1. Cup your hands and scrape the area where you feel cold, visualise there is a burning cauldron kept next to you, after scraping the area, throw the scraped waste into the burning cauldron. Repeat thrice. (This is just visualisation).

or

2. Visualize pulling out strands of hair from the cold areas, one by one, then tie a knot to the strands of hair and throw it into the universe.

Else

3. Visualise a bucket of salt water kept next to you. Do no. 1 above, and throw it into the bucket with the salt water instead of the burning cauldron.

By adopting any one of the above techniques, you will feel the cold areas are becoming warmer.
Continue with the Reiki session.

13

Visual Meditation Exercise:
The Glass Technique*

*T*he glass of water technique is a mental technique that can be used for problem solving and goal achievement. This technique is mostly taught in the Silva mind control classes.

As a graduate in the Silva mind control, I have personally studied and practised this technique and can promise you one thing — *IT WORKS.*

Whenever you come across a hurdle, a problem, that cannot be crossed or solved, do the following:

> At night just before retiring fill a glass of water and take it to the bed. When you are about to go off to sleep, cup the glass in your palms. Look for 30 seconds into the water in the glass. Repeat 'I know I have (state the problem)' — then close your eyes, look towards the ceiling of the room. Now repeat mentally: 'This is all I need to do to find the solution to the problem I have in my life.'

Drink half the water.

Cover the other half and keep aside.

In the morning when you wake up, before doing your routine chores, take the half-filled glass in your hands, repeat your problem mentally, and say: "Today, I will find the solution to my hurdle/problem." Drink the balance half of the water.

---

* As explained in Silva mind control classes.

What will happen is this:

Anytime during the day that follows, a message may be conveyed to you by anyone, your favourite TV soap opera; conversation with a friend, a thought from yonder; a remark passed by a friend. Anything. Just be on the look out.

Just in case nothing follows repeat the exercise again the next night — it works like magic.

Good luck.

14

Colours for Health

Red : Unlimited energy, used in cases of blood diseases

Orange : Digestion and assimilation of oxygen through the respiratory system, particularly in cases of asthma and diseases involving the lungs and chest area.

Yellow : For purification and also for diseases such as diabetes and those affecting the intestines and bowels.

Green : Revitalising the nervous and circulatory system and also the heart.

Blue : Tranquillity and peace, also used for destruction of all forms of infections.

Indigo : Treatment of all illnesses and diseases affecting the area of the head, the eyes, the ears and the nose, mostly for treatment of mental and emotional disorders.

Violet : Regeneration of the nervous system, for curing insomnia, mental disorders resulting from brain damage, physical illness and injury affecting the brain and diseases and injuries to the eyes.

| White | : | Unlimited energy for the treatment of all diseases and injuries. Treats the body and mind as a whole and is specially useful when a specific diagnosis of the individual's sickness for injury has not or cannot be made. |
| Blue-Green | : | For reduction of pain. |

COLOURS TO BE AVOIDED IN CERTAIN SITUATIONS

Red	:	If emotionally upset, hysterical or extremely overtired. The vital energies present in this colour can overload an individual with too much energy and make sought-after tranquillity more difficult to achieve.
Grey	:	If emotionally depressed. In situations where an individual has allowed himself/herself to give in to negativism concerning health or a situation of life, Grey should be totally avoided.
Blue	:	By individuals who find themselves depleted in physical or mental energies. When the physical, emotional or mental energy levels are low, blue in clothing or surrounds should be avoided.

15

The 'OM' Meditation

*E*ach day, just before the session of Reiki comes to an end, a short simple meditation of 30 seconds to one minute is to be carried out.

1. All students stand up and form a close circle.
2. All hands are to be put on the shoulders of students standing on the right and left side of you.
3. Close your eyes.
4. Chant "OM" (Actual sound AHHHHHHH...... UHHHHHHHH......OHHHHHH to end in a vibratory MMMMMMMMMM)
5. The chant is to be repeated thrice.

This is the OM meditation.

16

Summary

*W*hat we have learnt so far can be divided into three parts.

Part 1 is the visual meditation exercises that help us in treating this world and the people living in it with the white light meditation. The lily pond teaches us to remove our negativities and clean ourselves of all diseases. The glass technique teaches us to get the answers from yonder. Be alert, this technique says.

Part 2 is the Art of Living by Dr. Goenka where we learn to harness our bitterest enemy — *OUR ANGER* — in three ways: One, by diverting our attention, and using this energy creatively. Two, by mentally detaching ourselves and putting it in perspective and staring it down/viewing it. Three, slowing the agitated breath and thereby calming the sensations. Also, the OM meditation helps to subdue our ego, our desires and calm our nerves.

The colours teach us many things: what we wear, what we eat, what friends we have, speak a lot about us. Make it a prime factor in your lives and see the difference it makes.

Reiki — the chakras — we have learnt to give Reiki through the chakras, via, self-healing technique. The chakras harmonise our body. The most important thing to remember is the colour of each chakra. Mix the wrong colour and it will bring a major disaster in your life.

No questions are being asked at this stage, but tomorrow after completing the Reiki 1 session, we shall have some questions, which I am sure you will be able to answer spontaneously.

Part II

Reiki 1: Day 2

1

Reiki 'A' on 'B' and 'B' on 'A'

*W*hen you start giving Reiki to a person, you have to repeat the following:

For attitude and for gratitude:
I thank myself for being here.
I thank Reiki for being here.
I thank (insert the name of the person being treated) for being here.

Visualise a cloud above your head. Visualise the cloud emitting white light over you. Feel the white light travelling from your crown chakra to your third eye chakra, from your third eye chakra to your throat chakra and from your throat chakra to your heart chakra. Visualise the white light bouncing off from your heart chakra to your shoulders and from there flowing into your arms. Visualise the white light travelling from your arms into your palms. Visualise the white light emitting from your palms when you start giving Reiki.

Start Reiki.

REIKI 'A' ON 'B' — FRONT POSITIONS

Start with affirmations :

    For attitude & for gratitude
I thank myself for being here
I thank Reiki for being here
I thank (insert the person's name you are giving Reiki to) for being here

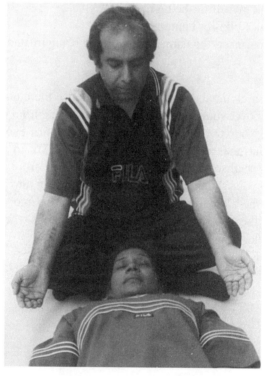

Fig - 1

   1) Sit as above
   2) Cover student in white light
   3) Cover yourself in white light
   4) Repeat mentally
      (a) I thank myself for being here
      (b) I thank Reiki for being here
      (c) I thank (patient's name) for
          being here.

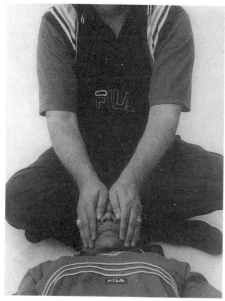

'Eyes'   Fig - 2

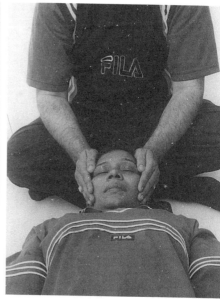

Temples   Fig - 3

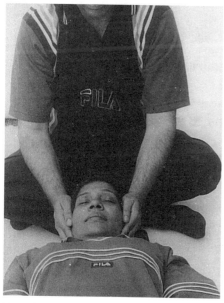

Ears   Fig - 4

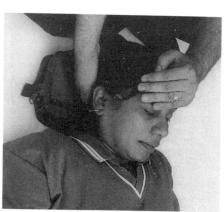

Front & Back of Head   Fig - 5

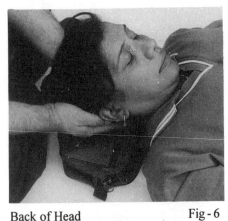

Back of Head   Fig - 6

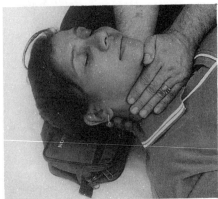

Front & Back of Throat Chakra   Fig - 7

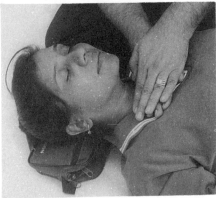

Thymus & Thyroid Glands   Fig - 8

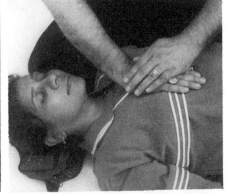

Heart Chakra   Fig - 9

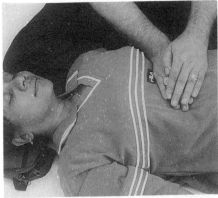

Solar Plexus   Fig - 10

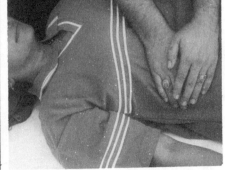

Liver   Fig - 11

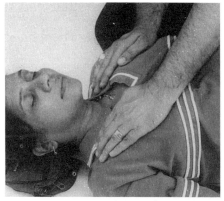

Shoulder Tips   Fig - 12

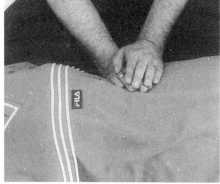

Pancreas & Spleen   Fig - 13

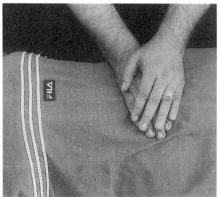

Hara   Fig - 14

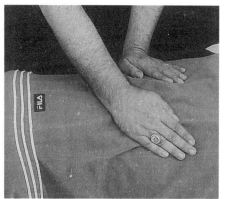

Ovaries   Fig - 15

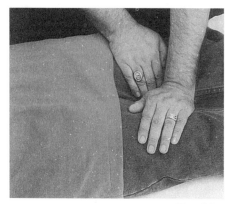

Thighs   Fig - 16

Knees   Fig - 17

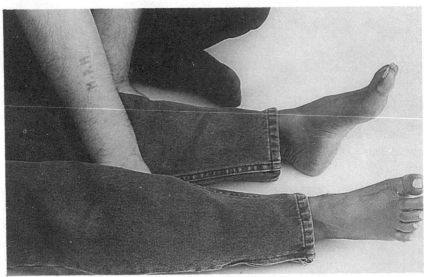

Calves   Fig - 18

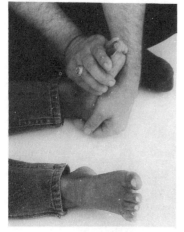

Left Foot   Fig - 19

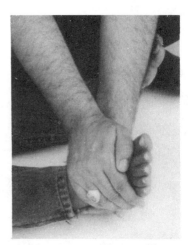

Right Foot   Fig - 20

SPIRALLING TECHNIQUE

First: Sit nearer to the centre of the body of the patient.

Next follow these four steps using the index and middle finger of your right hand, close the balance three fingers, and start drawing small anti-clockwise spirals 2" diametre. The fingers should not be more than 1" to 2" away from the body:

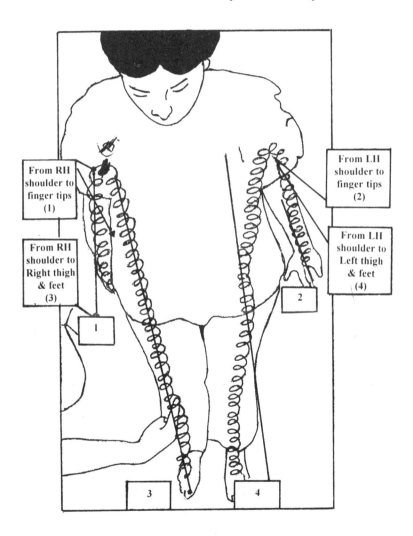

From RH shoulder to finger tips (1)

From LH shoulder to finger tips (2)

From RH shoulder to Right thigh & feet (3)

From LH shoulder to Left thigh & feet (4)

(1) From right shoulder downward to the arms and finger tips letting the flow end upward.
(2) From left shoulder downward to the arms and finger tips letting the flow end upward.
(3) From right shoulder downward to the right thigh and feet letting the flow end upward.
(4) From left shoulder downward to the left thigh and feet letting the flow end upward.

All spirals are to be repeated twice.

After spiraling request the patient to turn and lie down on the stomach.

THE BACK POSITIONS 'A' ON 'B'

Continue Reiki on the back positions:

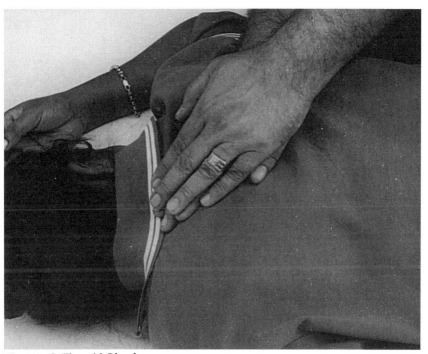

Thymus & Thyroid Glands
(Back side)

Fig - 21

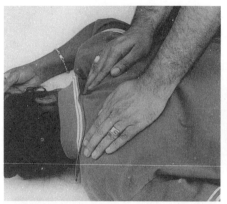

Shoulder Blades   Fig - 22
(Back side)

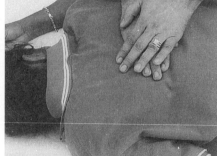

Heart   Fig - 23
(Back side)

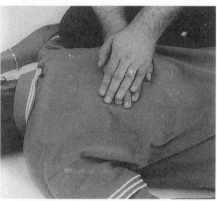

Solar Plexus   Fig - 24
(Back side)

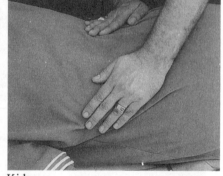

Kidneys   Fig - 25
(Back side)

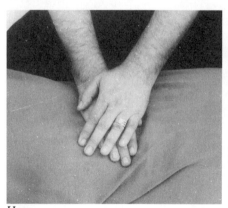

Hara   Fig - 26
(Back side)

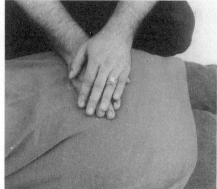

Root Chakra   Fig - 27
(Back side)

Let's Learn the Technique of "Chakra Balancing"

We have already studied that there are 7 main Chakras in the body. Their placements are :

(1) Crown — about 3" from the top of head.

(2) 3rd Eye — between eyebrows.

(3) Throat — on Adam's apple.

(4) Heart — on heart.

(5) Solar Plexus — above navel cord.

(6) Sexual — below navel cord OR on genitals.

(7) Root — At base of spinal cord.

(i)   RH on Crown Chakra.
(ii) LH on Root Chakra.

About 2" to 3" above body.

Fig - 1

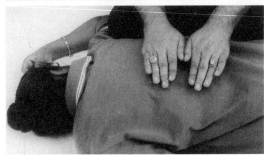

Both hands move slowly
to meet at Heart Chakra.

Fig - 2

Move to Fig. 1 position
Now move
    (i)   RH on 3rd Eye Chakra.
    (ii) LH on Sexual Chakra.

    About 2" to 3" above body.

Fig - 3

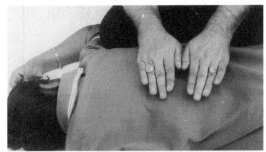

Both hands move
to meet at Heart Chakra.

Fig - 4

Move to Fig. 3 position
Now move
    (i)   RH on Throat Chakra.
    (ii) LH on Solar Plexus.

    About 2" to 3" above body.

Fig - 5

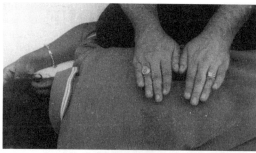

Both hands move to
meet at Heart Chakra.

Fig - 6

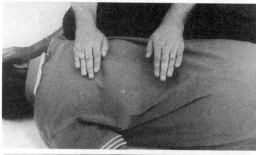

Move to Fig. 5 position
Now move
    (i)   RH on Crown Chakra.
    (ii) LH remains on Solar Plexu

About 2" to 3" above body.

Fig - 7

Both hands move to
meet at Heart Chakra.

Fig - 8

Move to Fig. 7 position
Now move
    (i)   LH moves to meet RH
        at Heart Chakra.

About 1" to 3" from body.

Fig - 9

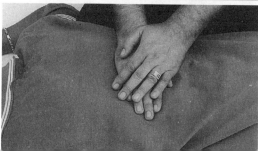

LH covers RH.
Pressurize slightly.

Fig - 10

THE STROKING TECHNIQUE

Point out the middle three fingers of your right hand and fold the small finger and the thumb into your palms.

Place the three fingers on the patient's throat and with a slight pressure pull it downwards towards the hara and/or root chakra — do this thrice.

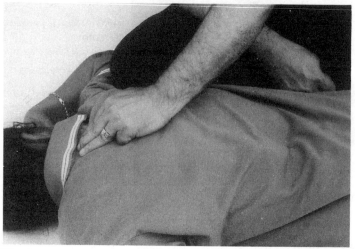

Fig - 1

(i) Three fingers placed on the neck.
(ii) Quickly draw your hands down towards hara and/or root chakra — do this thrice.

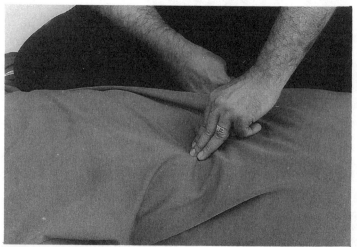

Fig - 2

THE CARESSING TECHNIQUE

Theory

Keep your left palm on the back of your right hand. Place this on the head and follow the diagram :

Your hands should not lose contact with the body and should move as described below:

(1) Covering head to right hand — from head to ears, shoulders, arms, elbow, wrist and fingers of right hand, move backwards the same way, come to head position.

(2) Covering head to left hand — from head to ears, shoulders, arms, elbow, wrist and fingers of left hand, move backwards the same way, come to head position.

(3) Covering head to right foot — from head to shoulders, waist, thighs, knees, calves, feet and move backwards the same way.

(4) Covering head to left foot — from head to shoulders, waist, thighs, knees, calves, feet and move backwards the same way.

(5) From head to heart chakra — stop — press slightly.

This completes the caressing technique.

This is Reiki "A" on "B"

Now you lie down, and the person who has taken Reiki will treat you. This will be Reiki "B" on "A"

The treatment will be exactly as "A" on "B"

2

Serious Cases

*A*s a Reiki channel at times you will be called to treat cases which are of a serious nature.

What do you do?

Accept these cases. Advise the next of kin of this people, tell them what Reiki is, the nature of Reiki and how the treatment is effected.

Advise them that as the person is in a serious condition, no guarantees on his life can be given. Be honest, but do not be negative. Tell the next of kin of the patient that you are not to be held responsible if anything untoward happens. In most of the Western countries, you may be taken to court.

Reiki is not a mumbo-jumbo practice. It is universal energy. Reiki passes through every problematic area into the body and heals the person by itself. We cannot control this energy.

For the first few days, there may be no results. Then from the fifth day onwards the patient may show some positive signs. Most probably around 12th to 14th day or so, the toxins start leaving the body, hence the patient may have a relapse.

Do not get worried; continue with the Reiki sessions.

Group therapy in these types of cases works wonders.

Reiki may be given to the patient for one and a half hours by each group of four to six people continuously for six to nine hours daily.

Do not worry about results, as Reiki is a positive and an intelligent energy. Think positive and hope for the best that the results will be positive.

3

Group Healing

Group healing is ideal for chronic diseases like cancer, AIDS, asthma, arthritis, diabetes, chronic rheumatism, lumbago, fever and blood related-problems, etc.

A group may consist of four to six Reiki channels treating the patient at one time.

Usually the most experienced person may take over the charge of the Reiki channels, but anyone who takes over the head position is considered to be the person in-charge for that particular session.

We have studied that there are 19 positions on the front side of the body, if the thighs, the knees and the calves are taken as one position each.

If the thighs, knees and the calves are taken separately then there are 22 positions on the front side of the body and 7 positions on the back side.

The person taking over the head position usually works out a chart.

Supposing you are the head person, how would you work out a chart?

First, how many other Reiki channels are present including you?

Supposing six.

How many total Reiki positions are there in the front side...?
Total 19 (taking the thighs, knees and calves as one position each).

As you are taking the head position, and there are five positions in that area (eyes, temples, ears, forehead, back of head) first we have to minus these five positions from the total of 19 positions. Balance positions left are 14 only.

Because the root chakra is equally important to the crown chakra, we leave one person to do the feet, as these are counted to be the extensions ruled by the root chakra. That is two positions. This will again leave a balance of 12 positions to be divided amongst the four people.

We have already placed two people,

1 — at the head
1 — at the feet

The other 4 will be seated as follows:

Person No. 1:   On the right hand side — will take the throat chakra, the lung tips, thymus and thyroid glands.

Person No. 2:   On the left side and will take the Heart Chakra, Solar Plexus and liver.

Person No.3:   On the right side and will take the Pancreas/ Spleen, Hara, Spermatical Cords/Ovaries.

Person No.4:   On the left side and will take the thighs, knees and calves.

All Reiki channels raise their hands, palms facing upwards and say the "Attitude of Gratitude"

For attitude and for gratitude
I thank (state your name here) for being here
I thank Reiki for being here
I thank (state the name of the patient) for being here.

The Reiki music cassette is played. On sound of the bell the hand positions are changed. All the Reiki channels know their positions beforehand. As some of the Reiki channels have less positions and some more, the ones having less positions will stop at the last position and continue giving Reiki to that part till the others complete their positions.

The person on the head position will do the spirals for the front side.

For the backside there are only seven positions,

(1) The person on the head position can take the shoulders and thymus/thyroid glands.

(2) The second person — the heart chakra.

(3) The third person — the solar plexus.

(4) The fourth person — the kidneys.

(5) The fifth person — the hara.

(6) The last person — the base of the spine (root chakra).

Again, the person in the head position will complete the session with the chakra balancing, the stroking and the caressing.

This completes the chapter on group healing.

4

Visual Meditation Exercise:
Your Sanctuary

*H*uman life is a daily struggle. There comes a day when you are frustrated, disillusioned, finding that you are at the lowest ebb of your life, you are frantic ...

And in this state you want one thing ... *TO GET AWAY FROM IT ALL.*

You seek a place, where you are alone with yourself. You do not want any outside force to ever see you again. You wish to be just alone, in a *SECRET PLACE*, which only you know of.

But, is there such a place?

Let's approach this from a different angle. But, before we do so, let me ask you a question. Okay?

● Which is the fastest mode of transport?

Think before you can answer.

I will answer this one for you: The fastest mode of transportation is your "*IMAGINATION*". In the beginning of the book, I have mentioned that the inner world is much bigger than the outside world. Comparatively, the outside world is smaller than the inside world.

So, why seek to hide on the outside. Why not take our imagination, our visualisation on the inside?

We create our own hiding spot, in the mountains, on any planet in the solar system, under the earth, above the earth, anywhere. But, this world of ours will be inside us. Nobody can find us there. We know how we expose ourselves to the world, clean, pious, and caring for others, but we also know what is inside us, don't we?

So, let's make a hiding place inside us. The ideas of the snow-clad mountains, forests, ponds, rivers and forests can be taken from the outside, but this world will be our world within us.

- Do your breathing exercise, breathe in to the count of 4, hold your breath to the count of 4, and breathe out to the count of 4.
- Continue with deep intakes of breath till you feel a little dizzy or till you feel relaxed.
- Visualise yourself in your favourite place of relaxation.
- Visualise you are taking a stroll in your favourite place of relaxation, where no other human being, animal or bird is allowed to enter without your permission.
- As you are strolling, visualise that there is a cloud following you.
- Look up at the cloud. This cloud looks great.
- Visualise that as you are looking at the cloud, the cloud bursts open and a force of white light descends on you.
- Feel as if millions of bulbs have been lighted up.
- Visualise the colours of the rainbow, violet, indigo, blue, green, yellow, orange, red, lilac, white.
- Feel the tingling sensations in your body.
- Feel as if you are being carried away on the wings of a big bird.
- You are feeling light, very light.
- All your worries, negativities, fears have been washed away by the light from the cloud.
- Mentally bow down and whisper, "I thank you Lord for the mercy shown to me, for giving me the power to fight back and rise up, thank you, thank you, thank you my lord"
- Look up at the cloud again, it has vanished.

- Keep strolling in your favourite place of relaxation.
- You do feel relaxed — isn't it?

Come back to the room as and when you feel you are ready to fight back and rise again.

5

When Not to Give Reiki

I recollect a case where a person had a major problem with the calves (legs). He was' overweight and was a chain smoker. He approached me for treatment. It is my habit to talk at length with the person requesting for Reiki. While counselling him, I came to know that this was a chronic problem he had.

He could never sit on a sofa or a chair for more than a few minutes. Everyday when he came home after the office hours, he would lie down on his back and keep his feet on the centre table for at least 30 minutes. He had tried every form of cure, but to no avail.

I started with the 21-day Reiki treatment and during the days that followed I felt his full body was cold. Sometimes, energy just wouldn't pass from my hands. He was not accepting energy. I was surprised. Then, on the ninth day, I visualised the valves of heart were clogged. I saw him gasping for breath. Then I saw him turn blue/greenish in colour. I started sweating. When I opened my eyes, he was smiling at me.

I stopped attending him. On the phone I advised him that something would happen. What, I had an idea but did not want to tell him about it at that time.

On the 12th day, he called me and said, "Do you know where I am sitting?" I was perplexed. He answered: "on the sofa". He paused, then continued: "Thank you very much for curing me. I have fired my family doctor. He could not cure me for the last eight years, and, you have shown me results in just nine days."

During the conversation I requested him to visit a cardiologist with me, I let out my fears on him and told him what I had visualised. He laughed.

Anyway, we went to the cardiologist. The cardiologist took X-ray and we found out his heart was enlarged. But, I knew this was not what I had seen. We attended another clinic, where the doctor showed me his valves on a TV screen. They were perfectly healthy.

But, the fear in me would not go.

On the 14th day of starting Reiki on him I got a call from him. Five days earlier I had stopped giving Reiki to him, as he was not accepting the energy. He just said: "I am sweating a lot and I am also feeling choked up". Intuitively, I knew it was a heart attack. I advised his friend who was with him, to call for an ambulance and rush him to a hospital.

I disconnected the line, called my friend's wife, advised her to rush to the hospital, and, took a cab myself to the hospital. My friend was brought on a stretcher and taken to the ICU. Within the next 25 minutes, he was pronounced dead.

The reason, I gave you the above incident is, anytime while treating a patient; you may come across a similar incident.

That is, while giving Reiki, you may feel that there is no energy passing through your hands, you may not feel any sensations, which you as a Reiki channel are supposed to feel.

When the soul is preparing to leave the body, it will not accept any energy from any source.

During these types of cases just excuse yourself and *DO NOT GIVE REIKI TO THAT PERSON.*

6

Visual Meditation Exercise: Your Counsellors

A time will come when you will seek advice from people around you asking questions:

- This person I am treating is suffering from throat cancer (optional), I am nervous, what if while giving Reiki, I catch the disease? Can you tell me what to do?
- I have been treating Mrs. XYZ for more than a month, but she doesn't seem to be responding. What shall I do?
- Mr. ABC coughs a lot when I give Reiki to him, I am nervous. What if I catch the virus and fall sick myself?
- Reiki is taking its own course, it takes a lot of time to heal, how can I heal the person faster?

Questions, questions and questions.

But, there are answers to every question. Aren't there?

Sometimes, we tend to ask questions to people who do not know the ABC of what we are doing. So, are they qualified to answer?

Sometimes, we tend to ask questions to qualified people, but those who do not know the language of meditation and healing techniques will scoff at these techniques. Are they qualified to answer our questions?

So, who is qualified? Who is the person who will appreciate the pains you are taking to heal people known and unknown to you? Who will listen to you patiently, discuss your problems with you. Who is the person in your mind whom you trust, whom you respect?

Select such two persons — One male and one female.

Now, as you have selected these two persons, we will do one more exercise.

- Visualise yourself in your favourite place of relaxation.
- Visualise yourself sitting under the shade of a tree and remembering these persons we were talking about.
- Utter one of the person's names on your lips. Visualise that person. See him standing in front of you.
- In this place, you do not need to speak, telepathy works here.
- Give way to your thoughts. Request this person, whom you cherish, respect and love, to become your counsellor. Request him you need his advice on matters pertaining to the sickness of the people, their depressions, their mental, spiritual, physical problems, which at times you fail to understand.
- Look out for the first thought. If it is "YES", he is chosen to be your counsellor. If "NO" look out for another person.
- Repeat the same with the other person — request her to be your counsellor.
- Look out for the first thought. If it is "YES", she is chosen to be your counsellor. If "NO" look out for another person.
- Relax — come back to the room whenever you feel like.

These counsellors will always help you with your medical cases when you come across hurdles, which seem difficult to cross.

7

Visual Meditation Exercise: Your Laboratory

*P*lease note that this is not a Reiki exercise.

We now have our secret place of relaxation.

We also have our own counsellors.

What happens when Reiki fails to cure?

When going through the Reiki course, I remember my Reiki teacher's wife was having a problem that Reiki could not cure. I was requested to ease the pain of this sweet and loving lady. I did what was necessary and she was excused from taking those 8/10-odd tablets she takes as her usual dosage.

What about Manjusha, she is also a Reiki master. Still she could not cure her mother's illness of frozen shoulders.

Maybe, my Reiki teacher and Manjusha are at fault, they talk about Reiki, my teacher teaches Reiki, but do they have the patience?

If they do, then Reiki is a failure, but, if not, then the system is not wrong, it is the people.

Maybe they are lacking in love and compassion for their fellow beings.

There are too many maybes. But, the choice is yours to decide.

To make the *ART OF HEALING COMPLETE*, I shall be teaching you three more arts during this Reiki course which shall make your healings complete.

You can treat anyone of any disease with 100 per cent results.

Coming back to this chapter, we may need to give treatments to the people in absentia. By absentia, I mean, when they are not physically present.

How do we do that?

Simple.

We make a UNIQUE LABORATORY, where we have all the treatment facilities that a human mind can conceive.

First, we do the normal breathing exercise.

Then, when we are feeling relaxed, we go to our favourite place of relaxation.

From here, we go to some place else and make a laboratory.

The Exercise

- Visualise yourself erecting a laboratory in your mind with your mental thoughts.
- Visualise yourself inside the main hall of this laboratory.
- Mentally call in your counsellors.
- Visualise your counsellors are in your presence.
- Mentally discuss with them what you need in this laboratory.
- Visualise yourself erecting a big screen.
- Mentally repeat the following: "By the power given to me by my Supreme Self, I instill the power in this screen, to show the places of defect in the human body when the person is placed behind it."
- Visualise a computer in front of you.
- Mentally repeat the following: "By the power given to me by my Supreme Self, I load this CPU with the most successful programmes on the healing techniques ever conceived by a human mind"
- Mentally converse with your counsellors requesting them to be present in this laboratory for 24 hours a day for the rest of their lives, inventing cures for diseases which the world has failed to cure.
- Visualise them smile and affirm to your request.
- Mentally, seek their permission to leave.
- Come back to the room whenever you feel you are ready to do so.

For this exercise, you have to be careful to do the following:

- Always wish your counsellors individually whenever you enter or leave the laboratory.
- Never think negatively when in the laboratory.
- There is a cure for every disease in this laboratory.
- The counsellors are always present in the laboratory to listen and to advise you.
- Your entry to the laboratory is always first, then if you wish you can call your patient.
- Discuss the patient with the counsellors first, then call the patient to this laboratory.
- Never, never, talk to the patient in the laboratory. Just treat him/her.
- In serious cases, the mental image can be left under a white light till further notice.
- Operations can be performed to the best of your and the counsellor's knowledge.
- While treating the heart, always remember to stop the clock. After the heart is treated, you can start the clock again.
- *NEVER, EVER*, touch the heart of a patient till the clock has been stopped.
- The clearer the mental pictures, the faster the treatments/ results will be.

8

Meditation

"**D**avid," I called out to one of my students during the Reiki classes.

"Yes," he tuned in.

"Can you tell me — what is meditation?"

"It is an art where you sit down doing nothing, and, the results are you achieve everything."

Bravo. I could not have explained better.

If you want the doors to be thrown open to you to plunge yourself into the world of light, the world of love, the world of truth, plunge yourself into meditation. Meditation will lead you to the ultimate goal of your existence and self-realisation.

The next natural question asked would be: How do we meditate?

We meditate in four different ways, similar to the wheels of a car.

(1) The first wheel is to focus on our inner self.
(2) The second wheel is the use of a mantra, a word or a syllable that assists in concentration.
(3) The third is an asana or the sitting posture that supports the body and stimulates the nervous system.
(4) The fourth wheel is the breath, balancing the twin process of inhalation and exhalation.

Let's divert ourselves a little. We talk about our relaxation — about sleep. When we feel sleep taking over us, we shy away from our wife, our children, food, TV ... everything that we believe gives us comfort. During our sleep, the weariness washes away and when we wake up, we feel completely relaxed. We experience this everyday. If we ponder on this subject, we will realise all the external activities we engage ourselves during the day exhaust us. But, the internal activity (sleep) rejuvenates us. So, eating, drinking, partying, TV are not the permanent pleasures that will bring us peace. When we sleep we are peaceful. During the day the mind turns outwards. However, in the sleep state, the mind takes some rest in the self, and, it is this that removes our fatigue. Absorbed in this little bliss of sleep, we forget the pains of the waking state. If we were to go just beyond sleep and enter into the state of meditation, we would be able to drink the nectar of love and happiness that lies in the heart.

This nectar is what we are looking for in all activities of the outer world. What we are really seeking is the supreme truth, and, through meditation we can experience this truth vibrating in the form of sublime happiness in the heart.

The truth is that you are divine and divinity is your birthright. Each of us is divinity packaged in bone and muscle. It is only the wrong understanding that keeps you small. We are distracted by the packaging. You think yourself as only a body. You think you are in a certain physical structure, with hands, feet, legs, eyes, ears, and mouth...

You differentiate yourself by sex — a man, a woman; by class; by race; by nationality. You identify yourself with your thoughts, your talents, your positive and your negative actions. But this is not what you are.

Within you is a being that knows all the actions of the body and the mind, and, remains untouched by all of them. The body is a temple, the being inside you is the keeper of the temple.

The one, who tends to the temple, has to be different from the temple. For example, you will say "my body" similar to "my wife", "my children", "my mother".

Your mother is different from you — hence my mother.
Your children have to be different from you — hence "my children".
Your wife has to be different from you — hence "my wife".
Your body has to be different from you — hence "my body".

Who is this keeper of your temple — your body who observes the activities of your waking hours? At night when you sleep, this keeper remains awake and reports to you the dreams you have had in the night. Who is this keeper?

The one who lives in the temple — your body, but who is apart from the body is YOUR REAL SELF. That self is beyond the body, beyond the mind, beyond distinctions of name, colour, sex, and nationality. It is the Pure "I", the Original "I" consciousness that has been with us since we came into this world.

What we have done is that we have superimposed different notions on to that "I" awareness.

The physical "I" constantly keeps changing. From I am a child to I am an adult, I am a brother, I am a son, I am a husband, I am a father, I am a grandfather; I am a clerk, I am a supervisor, I am an officer, I am a manager — the I keeps travelling through different phases all the time.

Meditation is concentration — concentration should be:

This "I" is not only pure consciousness but is also a form of bliss. It is the ABSOLUTE. That I — IS GOD and we meditate to know that directly. As we see and feel it more and more, we become more transformed.

Many techniques are being taught in this world and age to realise it. But, the oldest art is the art of meditation. Because, it is only in meditation that we see the inner self directly. That which lives in the heart cannot be found in the books. It cannot be found in any religion and neither can it be found in any religious books.

Remember, "All books are written by a brain, yes, the brain can make any number of books, but no book can make a brain". Better throw out the books and MEDITATE.

Meditation is universal. It does not belong to any cult or sect. It does not belong to the East or West, or to any religion. Meditation is everyone's property just like sleep is everyone's property, it belongs to humanity.

Everyone meditates. Doctors, cooks, teachers, painters, mothers and everyone else.

Any type of concentration on any particular field is known as meditation though this meditation is external.

What we have to do is to meditate internally. What does meditation do?

- It rids us of disease and makes us more skillful at everything we do.
- Understanding of inner and outer things becomes steadily deeper.
- Stills the mind which constantly wanders.
- We travel to different inner worlds and have innumerable inner experiences.
- Relieves us of our sufferings.
- Establishes us forever in the state of supreme peace.
- Makes us aware of our own true nature.
- On a particular object in order to still and focus the mind.
- One can concentrate on the heart.
- On the open space between the eyebrows — third eye chakra.
- On any being who has risen above passion and attachment.
- Wherever the mind finds satisfaction.

The best being the inner self. Don't we need to know our inner self first? Don't we need to experience our self? Remember the Bible: "What you seek you get". Seek thy inner self and it shall be thine.

When you sit for meditation, do not worry about thoughts evading your privacy. Do not try to erase the thoughts in the mind. Accept them. These thoughts are nothing but consciousness itself.

Let the mind wander as much as it wants to; do not try to subdue it. Witness the thoughts that arise in you. Be aware of the thoughts coming to you. This is but a play of your consciousness. You are also a play of your own consciousness. Hence, the thoughts are nothing but you.

You need a thorn to take out a thorn from your body. Another way to meditate is to put a thought into your mind to avoid the other thoughts from entering your conscious/sub-conscious level. The thought that you are going to use is a "mantra".

Either the mantra will be a one-word syllable like:

"OM"
"AING"
"REEM"
"JEEM"

Or a sentence. Or any positive affirmation can also be treated as a mantra:

"If God be for me, who can be against me?"
"Day by day in every way I am becoming better and better and better."

Mantra is a thought that redeems and protects the one who contemplates it. Mantra is the heartbeat of meditation — the greatest of all techniques. Mantra is self-vibration, self-speech, and when we immerse ourselves into the mantra, it leads us to the place of the self.

Mantra repetition should be with reverence during meditation; it begins to work within. This energises us and awakens our inner energy, our own power.

What should be our physical posture when we sit in the mantra meditation?

There are four postures in which meditation can be done.

1. The lotus posture (in yoga this is known as *padmasan*).
2. The half lotus posture (in yoga this is known as *siddhasan*).
3. The easy posture (in yoga this is known as *sukhasan*).
4. The lying down position (in yoga this is known as *shavasan*).

The most important of the above is the lotus position. Because by sitting in this position for a period of one-and-a-half hours, the 72,000 nerves and inner subtle channels get purified. Moreover, the mind will begin to turn inward and meditation will happen on its own.

Breathing should be natural and spontaneous. We must not try to disturb the natural rhythm of the breath. The mind and the breath work in conjunction with each other. So let the rhythm of your breathing be natural. As you repeat the mantra, the breath will go in and out in time with the rhythm of the mantra and will become steady by itself.

Meditation on the self is very easy. All that we really need are love and interest. As we meditate more and more, the inner power awakens and begins to unfold.

The inner universe is greater than the outer universe; it is so vast that the entire outer cosmos can be kept in just one corner of it. Everything is contained within it, and that is why, in meditation, the seers were able to discover all the secrets of the universe.

Within us are infinite miracles, infinite wonders. As we go deeper into meditation, we will come to understand the reality of all the different inner worlds we read about in the scriptures. Within these inner spaces, nectarine music resounds. Within us are such delicious nectars that nothing in this world can compare with them in sweetness. We should meditate systematically and with great persistence and go deeper and deeper within the body. In this way, meditation will be a gradual unfolding of our inner being.

Along the way there will be many experiences. But, the true state is beyond them. As we go deeper into meditation, we reach a place where we see nothing and hear nothing. Here there is nothing but bliss. This is the place of the self, and, true meditation is to become immersed in that!

From the book *Meditation*

9

Reiki: What We Have Learnt So Far

*W*e have travelled a long way. From knowing nothing to knowing something — is achieving a lot. Whatever knowledge we gain will certainly improve our status, our being, ourselves.

What are the important things we have learnt so far?

(1) The white light meditation to make this world a better place to live in.

(2) The meaning and the history of Reiki.

(3) The five principles of Reiki.

(4) How to control the devil in you — your anger — by a discourse by Dr. Goenka in the Art of Living.

(5) The Chakras.

(6) The Reiki positions.

(7) The colours for health and their effect on our daily lives.

(8) How to give a complete session of Reiki.

(9) Group healing.

(10) Apart from Reiki, we have made our own place of relaxation; we have our own counsellors and our own laboratory, which we shall use to treat people by the mind control and TV - Pic methods.

(11) We had a very good discourse on meditation and the art of meditation.

(12) Most important is that we have also learnt the art of visual meditation that gives us peace of mind and builds us up to become better humans.

10

It's Time for Examination

QUESTION PAPER

*Y*ou have worked wonders with yourself. You have been working hard to reach this far. How do you feel at this time and hour? Do you feel satisfied internally? Do you want to know if you are successful? If yes, please answer the following questions:

(1) What is Reiki?

(2) Why do Reiki masters/teachers always have the white light meditation included in their seminars?

(3) What are the five principles of Reiki?

(4) Why did Dr. Usui Mikao adopt the five principles of Reiki?

(5) How many positions are there on the front side of the body and how many on the back side of the body, please mention their names also.

(6) What is Reiki Alliance and who started the Reiki Alliance?

(7) What would you do when you come across cold areas while giving Reiki?

(8) What is group healing?

(9) Give a chart of six people giving a group healing to a patient. State briefly how the positions will be divided amongst each person on the front side of the body and on the back side of the body.

(10) Did you try to do any visual meditation exercises? If yes, which one. What was the outcome of it? What did you feel? How did you feel after completing the exercise?

(11) Did you do the attunements? Who did the attunements for
      you? What was your experience during Day 1? Also, what
      was your experience during Day 2?
(12) Do you feel your palms are getting warmer than usual? If
      yes, then what do you think the reason is?

A REIKI 1 CERTIFCATE will be issued to you if you can
answer the above questions and post it to:

Mohan Makkar.
c/o UBS Publishers' Distributors Ltd.
5 Ansari Road, Daryaganj,
New Delhi-110 002 (India)

Please ensure the certificate is duly filled in to suit your
requirements.

The REIKI 1 CERTIFICATE will be posted to you in
45 days' time if the questions are found to have been answered
satisfactorily. If the questions have not been answered
satisfactorily, we will advise you accordingly.

You will also be complemented with the Reiki 2 Attunement
Booklet, which will take you to the advance level of Reiki 2.

USUI SHIKI RYOHO

THIS IS TO CERTIFY THAT

has attained the **FIRST DEGREE** in
the REIKI method of Natural Healing.

Date _____

Place _____

MOHAN MAKKAR

TRADITIONAL REIKI MASTER

INDEPENDENT TEACHER OF REIKI

Part III

Reiki 2: Day 1

1

Let's Discuss Your Self-Healing/ Reiki Experience

*W*elcome back to the advance level of Reiki 2.

For those of you who are new to this seminar on Reiki 2, I would like to introduce myself. My name is Mohan. I will be your Reiki master/teacher during these two-and-a-half days' seminar.

Before we proceed further, I would like to congratulate you all present for successfully completing the Reiki 1 course.

The question is: Did you complete the "21 days" self-treatment?

If the answer is 'yes', you may stay back.

For those who have not done the "21 days" self-treatment — please leave this room.

What did you feel during the last "21 days" of giving Reiki to yourself?

How do you feel now?

Do you feel you are ready for Reiki 2?

I can see the smiles on some of your faces. You look calmer, more peaceful with yourself. Good.

Keep giving Reiki to yourself — not only will your body become healthy, your mental powers will increase and so will be your attitude towards life. To put it in a nutshell — *YOU WILL BE A BETTER PERSON.* Let's discuss — why we need to do the Reiki 2 course?

2

Why Second Degree — A Discussion

*T*he ones who are remaining here presumably have completed the 21 days of self-cleansing. By self-cleansing I mean all of you must have gone through giving Reiki to yourselves for a period of 21 days.

Some of you may have given Reiki to other people also. How many of you have given Reiki to others?

All?

Good. Could you diagnose the ailments while giving Reiki? Where you accurate in your diagnosis?

How did you feel by becoming a Reiki channel?

Of course, you must have felt nice, otherwise you wouldn't be here, isn't it?

I am sure some of you must have felt inadequate. Let me clarify.

Some of you must have been approached by family members/friends/acquaintances to treat people who are not physically present. In these circumstances, I am sure you must have felt insufficient.

Do not worry. The reason for doing Reiki 2 is simple.

We learn Reiki in a wider way. By the time this seminar ends, you will be self-sufficient to treat any case, be it physically or in absentia. You will learn to treat all types of diseases. You will also learn to give short form of Reiki. You will become adept at the absentee healing techniques using the tools of Reiki, mind control, colours, and crystals. You will also be doing more visual meditation exercises that are serious in nature.

To learn Reiki 1 was a pleasure. To learn Reiki 2 will be a pleasure-cum-business for you. You remember that one of the principles of Reiki is the attitude for gratitude. Anyone you treat should be charged. An act of gratitude for the Reiki given. Charged in the sense not of monetary benefits. If the person taking Reiki from you cannot afford to pay you, and you know he is incapable, request him to bake a cake for you, to cook any one dish for you. That person at a later date can run some chores for you, as long as the attitude of gratitude is attained.

In the being when I first did my master/teacher degree, I charged US$40.00 per treatment. I even charged my students to teach Reiki.

I was told never to reveal the symbols. But, then I start thinking deeply.

- I reveal the symbols to people who pay me, don't I.
- I revealed the secrets of attunements for people who did the master/teacher degree course with me, didn't I.

Is this energy mine or yours? Or is this energy some private property?

This is THE UNIVERSAL ENERGY.

Universal energy should belong to the universe. To the people living in it. So, why not give this wonderful gift to the people.

Most of the Reiki masters/teachers I know charge the sky for teaching these techniques. Teach but do not sell them. Teachers are not business people.

It is only education that will always multiply when given away. Just like a smile, it will multiply and come back to you.

Hence, make sure, even if you have to take a pence or a cent for your treatment, accept it with the attitude of gratitude, but treat that person.

Hence, to complete the extent of your reach in the treatment of diseases, Reiki 2 is necessary.

3

The Three Reiki Symbols

THE FIRST REIKI SYMBOL

What Dr. Usui found in the Tibetan sutras were four symbols, three of which are taught in the Reiki 2 class and the strongest one is taught in the Reiki 3A class. That is the reason the 3A Reiki is known as the Reiki Master Degree.

Of these three symbols — the first one is:

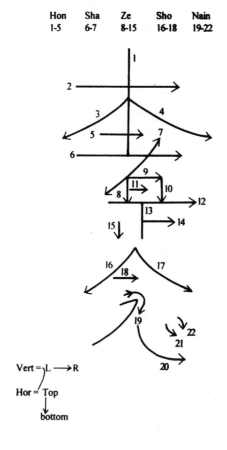

This symbol is pronounced as "Hon (Hohhn) Sha (Shhaaah) Ze (Zay) Sho (Show) Nain (Nayn)

THE SECOND REIKI SYMBOL

The second Reiki symbol is drawn as follows:

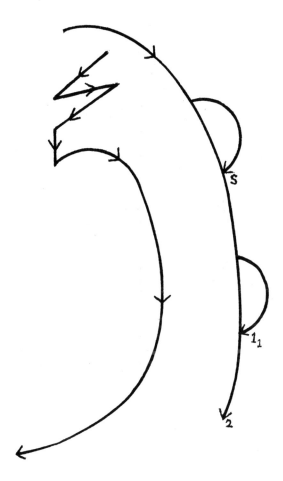

This is pronounced as "Say Hay Ki".

THE THIRD REIKI SYMBOL

This symbol is drawn as follows:

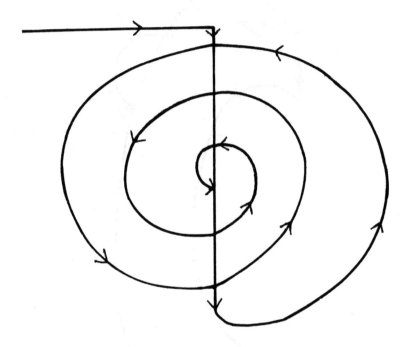

The pronunciation is : "Cho (Chohh) Ku (Kooooo) Ray (as in "Ray")

SOME OTHER SYMBOLS

   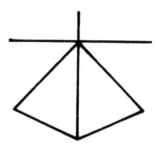

The Heart Centre Symbol   **The Harth Symbol**

The Zonar Symbol   **The Halu Symbol**

4

What to Do with These Symbols?

During the Reiki classes that I conduct, I give the three symbols to my students, tell them to trace the first symbol with their forefinger. They do it over and over again. Then I tell them to trace this symbol from memory. Usually they do it at the first try. I have never seen any student fail to draw this symbol in less than 10 minutes — maximum.

In a similar way the second symbol and the third symbol are taught. Compared to the first symbol, the second and third symbols are very easy to draw.

The third symbol — "*CHO KU RAY*" — and the second symbol "*SAY HAY KI*" are mostly used for curing the cold areas.

Remember the three techniques to cure the cold areas? Yes, the shovelling and throwing bad energy into the cauldron, the threading and throwing into the universe and shovelling and throwing into a bucket with salt water.

These symbols are created for the same purpose. Now, when the cold areas are met with, you shovel and do the same as taught in Reiki 1, but, at the same time, repeat the mantras — either "CHO KU RAY" or "SAY HAY KI".

Whichever mantra enters your mind first should be repeated thrice.

MEANINGS & FUNCTIONS OF SYMBOLS

HON SHA ZE SHO NEN

HON	The centre, the essence, the source, the beginning, the start out of itself.
SHA	Shining
ZE	To walk in the right direction
SHO	The goal, aim, honest being
NEN	Silence, to be open in the deepest being of your nature (who you are)

The purpose of this symbol is to bring down the energy into your Heart Chakra, open the mind so that Reiki can operate beyond time and space.

Hon Sha Ze Sho Nen acts as a bridge for energy to flow. Though important particularly in Absent Healing, it is used always.

SEI HE KI

SEI	State of embryo, things which are invisible, source of external form.
HE KI	Root Chakra to be balanced.

Sei He Ki breaks through or breaks down those which are not in harmony. It breaks through our blockages and patterns on the aura level, emotional level and physical level and establish their harmony.

CHO KU REI

CHO	Curved sword (sickle) which draws a curved line
KU	To enter something and produce wholeness, to produce space where nothing exists.
REI	Spiral, essence, mystical power, that which is not explanatory.
Cho Ku Rei	Is the power symbol used for amplification of energy. It is a catalyst and activator.

Now, when you start giving Reiki to the patient, you start with the attitude of gratitude:

I thank myself for being here,
I thank Reiki for being here,
I thank (name of the patient) for being here

After this the first thing you do is to place your cupped hands on the eyes of the patient. In Reiki 1 you just played the Reiki cassette and awaited the sound of the bell. In Reiki 2, you start mentally drawing the first symbol through your third eye chakra on the right eye of the patient. After the complete symbol has been drawn, repeat mentally, "Hon Sha Zay Sho Nayn" thrice.

Through your third eye chakra, mentally draw the second symbol on the right eye. After the complete symbol has been drawn, repeat mentally, "Say Hay Ki" thrice.

Do the same with the third symbol.

Now, repeat this exercise on the left eye.

To summarise the above briefly: the three symbols (1) Hon Shah Zay Sho Nain, (2) Say Hay Ki and (3) Cho Ku Ray are to be drawn on every position your hand covers as shown in the table. (See following page).

Points to Remember:

- When I say a full set, it means each mantra drawn once, repeated thrice on a single position.
- On the table the number of positions are mentioned. A full set is to be done on each position.
- After the feet, do not forget to do the spirals.
- After the base of the spine is over, do not forget to do the chakra balancing, the caressing and the stroking.
- Draw each mantra from the third eye chakra to the hand in position and repeat the mantra mentally.

PART	POSITIONS
EYES	2
TEMPLES	2
EARS	2
FOREHEAD/BACK	2
BACK OF HEAD	1
THROAT CHAKRA	2
THYMUS/THYROID GLANDS	1
HEART CHAKRA	1
SOLAR PLEXUS	1
LIVER	1
LUNG TIPS,	2
PANCREAS/SPLEEN	1
HARA	1
SPERMATIC CORDS (GENTS)	2
OVARIES (LADIES)	1
THIGHS (RIGHT) & (LEFT)	2
KNEES (RIGHT) & (LEFT)	2
CALVES (RIGHT) & (LEFT)	2
ANKLE & SOLE OF FOOT (RIGHT)	1
ANKLE & SOLE OF FOOT (LEFT)	1
BACK - SHOULDERS	2
BACK - THYMUS & THYROAD GLANDS	1
BACK - HEART CHAKRA	1
BACK - SOLAR PLEXUS	1
BACK - KIDNEYS	2
BACK - HARA	1
BACK - BASE OF SPINE	1

5

Chanting of Symbols

*A*fter learning the Reiki symbols, I make it a practice to ensure that we do the following exercise:

- We sit in a circle.
- One student gets into the circle.
- Excluding the one in the circle, all others start chanting "Hon Sha Zay Sho Nain".
- The student in the centre visualises the symbol in the front of the third eye chakra, while the others are chanting the first mantra.
- The second mantra is chanted "Say Hay Ki".
- The student in the centre visualises the symbol in the front of the third eye chakra, while the others are chanting the second mantra.
- The third mantra is chanted "Cho Ku Ray".
- The student in the centre visualises the symbol in the front of the third eye chakra, while the others are chanting the third mantra.

We repeat this chanting with each student getting a chance to sit in the centre and visualise.

At the end of the session, we ask about the experiences from the students.

6

Introduction to Mind Control Healing

I had a very good experience sometime back. An Irish girl Norma paid me a visit. She had completed her course from another Reiki teacher, and things were happening to her. She was passing through a phase where she needed help and assistance.

She called her Reiki teacher to help her during her healing crises. She did not get any help from her Reiki teacher.

I usually advertise in the local magazines, and, Norma picked up my name from the magazine. She called me and asked for help. I asked her what help she needed?

She replied: "I am in a trauma, tell me Mr. Mohan, are the mind and the brain same thing?"

I replied in the affirmative, but she was not convinced. Then going over the books I found some articles on the brain, meditation. Adding part of my knowledge to this I made an article for her that is presented to you:

Dear Norma,

As requested by you. In return of your mind (brain?) boggling question: Are the mind and the brain same?

I am not an authority on this subject, neither is science my forte. But, I have tried my best to answer your question as clearly and as honestly as possible.

Scientists have identified four basic types of brain (physical) waves:

1. Beta
2. Alpha
3. Theta
4. Delta

These correspond to the four levels of brain activity.

In Delta you produce brain waves of one half to four cycles per second (CPS). It is the zone of deep, unconscious sleep, a little known area of total unawareness.

In Theta, you produce from five to seven CPS. This is the zone of deep, comfortable sleep, an area of complete and utter satisfaction.

In Alpha you produce from 8 to 13 CPS, alpha is the area of relaxing sleep and dreaming, sometimes also called the REM (rapid eye movement) because eyes flicker rapidly when you are dreaming.

In Beta, the outer conscious aware state, your brain produces waves of from 14 to 40 CPS. At the moment you are reading this article you are in Beta.

The average person, at an average time, during an average day, is in the Beta area producing 21 CPS (actually the brain produces all four segments simultaneously; the amplitude, consistency, and frequency of waves determine the predominant area of activity).

Good health, intelligence, concentration, ease, pure genius in the area of brain wave production that falls below 19 CPS.

Psychosomatic problems are simply problems caused by the mind (psyche) getting in the way of the body (soma). By relieving the body of the problems of the mind through the alpha-generated separation of the psyche and soma, physical problems often resolve themselves.

An easy way to achieve the alpha state of ten cycles per second is through the meditative process. Meditation has a rhythm all its own, as does excitement, or anger, or for that matter any emotion that either stirs one up or calms one down. What meditation does is to slow down the brain waves and separate the mind from the body. This enables the mind to concentrate better, since it does not have to deal with the body's nervous system or emotional manifestations, or its reactions to outer and inner stimuli.

As far as the body is concerned, without the mind to harass it, the bodily intelligence can do its work. Its main job is to keep the cells in an energised balance so that it can be stabilised in a healthy condition. The major health benefit of meditation, then, is keeping the mind from interfering with the body so both may do their respective jobs — the body healing itself when ill and remaining healthy when healthy.

Your question has been answered above.

The "mind" is defined as a "psyche" (as per Webster — Psyche is defined as "soul, self, mind") to go broader and deeper into the meaning of "soul and mind", we have the following definitions:

Soul : The immaterial essence, animating principle, or actuating cause of an individual life.(Abstract — cannot be seen).
The spiritual principles embodied in human beings. (Abstract — cannot be seen).
The quality that arouses emotions and sentiments. (Abstract — cannot be seen).

Mind : The element or complex of elements in an individual that feels, perceives, thinks, wills, and specially reasons (All abstracts — cannot be seen).

From the above it is conceived that the mind in all respects is "Abstract". It does not have a body, while the brain is physical, it is present, it can be seen.

Of course, the brain and the mind go hand in hand, encroaching on each other's territories so much that it appears as if they are one and the same.

By sitting in meditation, the mind is controlled, this in turn controls the thoughts, then breathing is controlled and the nervous system relaxes, in lieu of which the brain also relaxes. In conclusion of the above: It is my strongest belief that the brain and mind though they seem to be the same entity are not the same.

Hope I have been able to solve your dilemma.

Regards

Mohan Makkar

For any problems, you can always contact me on the usual phone nos.1 that you have.

Dated: 21/7/1997

I am sure you must have understood what is "mind control" from the above.

You can work wonders if you can visualise clearly with your third eye chakra being the centre of focus.

Once you have the art of controlling your thoughts, you can proceed with the alternate treatments:

Step 1:

- Pick up a patient you wish to treat.
- Analyse his/her sickness.
- Think how would a doctor heal this disease.
- Think how you would treat this disease — memorise it.

Step 2 (Points to Remember):

- Begin with visualisation.
- Go to your favourite place of relaxation.
- After relaxing a few moments, go to the laboratory.
- Wish each counsellor individually.
- Discuss the problems with the counsellors.

- As you already have the plan for treatment, see that the equipment is ready.
- Bring the person wanting treatment into the mental frame of your third eye chakra.
- Ask permission to heal thus "by the power given to me by my Supreme Self, I request your permission to treat you of (give the name of the disease)"
- If the answer is "yes" call him to your laboratory, where you go ahead with the treatment
- NEVER EVER treat a patient if permission by the Supreme Self is not granted or if you feel that the permission has not come through.
- On working near the chest or the heart area, create a mental clock, see it working, and then stop the clock. Proceed with treatment in the area. After the treatment is over, restart the mental clock.
- Always mentally wash your hands before and after the treatment.
- Do not talk with the patient.
- Depending on the chakra where the sickness is located, try and leave that particular colour in that area. If you do not understand, do not ponder, just leave a shiny white light in the area.
- Be swift and accurate, do not hesitate. Withdraw if you wish to, or, if you feel nausea, but before withdrawing cover that area in white light.
- After the treatment cover the patient in white colour and encircle him/her in white light. Make the patient float in white light and leave him there; visualising that he is smiling and happy.
- Say thank you to the Supreme Self of that person.
- Say thank you to your higher self.
- Say thank you to your counsellors — individually.
- Send the patient back to the place he had come from.

Note:

If you feel the person is having a chronic/major problem, do not let the person leave the laboratory. Leave the mental image under a post where he is immersed in the white light. Request your counsellors to take care that the white light does not go off.

Also instruct your supreme self to carry out the treatment which you have done, every six hours. What will happen is that though you may be consciously busy with your daily jobs, your subconscious mind will do the treatment every six hours.

Ensure you go to the laboratory and check on the patient at least every 24 hours.

If you are persistent and patient, result will surely follow.

7

The Sound Meditation

*D*uring many seminars conducted by me, discussions have always followed with students who claim "I can NEVER sit in meditation without a thought entering my mind for more than five seconds"

Accepted.

During one such discussion, I asked the lady, "What if you sit in meditation for five full minutes and not a single thought enters your mind?"

The lady was perplexed. FIVE MINUTES?

I smiled at her.

First of all I put on my television and increased the volume to moderately high. Next, I put on the FM music. Then, I opened the windows of the drawing room. (As my house is located near the main road, we could hear the sound of moving vehicles very clearly). Again, I took a piano from my daughter's toys and I started playing it.

There were mixtures of sounds in the room.

I told that lady and the other students in the room: "I give you all five minutes to count the number of sounds you hear". Then to bait them I added, "Whoever can count the maximum number of sounds will get a gift from me. The gift can be anything". Then after a pause I added, "Maybe a free master degree course".

Everybody was hooked.

I looked at my stopwatch. "START" I clicked my fingers.

There was silence in the room (by silence I mean — everyone of my students stopped talking and closed their eyes in concentration — meditation pose).

Five minutes slipped by. I was quiet. 6...............7
................8 .... 9 ....10.

I stopped playing the piano; I put off the FM radio; I put off the TV; I closed the window.

Slowly, one by one, the students opened their eyes.

Everyone was smiling. A naughty mischievous smile on the face.

I looked at them and said: "Okay — how many sounds"

"DAVID"
"48"

"MARC"
"17"

"ZUBAIR"
"72"

"MEENA"
"44"

"FLORA"
"84"

This was the lady who could not sit in meditation for more than five seconds before a thought entered her mind.

"NIGEL"
"33"

"And," I continued, "may I ask if any one of you had any thoughts?"

Not a single one.
100 per cent results.

I gave 50 per cent fees off for the lady with the 84 sounds for that particular course.

Now, whenever I contact them asking them of their progress in Reiki and meditation, I know that I have been successful with these students.

The sound meditation has become a most in-thing.

8

A Medipic Healing Exercise

Arthritis

1. Contact subconscious mind of the sufferer and talk gently.
2. Observe and identify all of the crystalline deposits on the bones of both hands.
3. Mentally separate each joint and with a nail file or emery board, clean the bones of all crystal deposits.
4. Before reassembling the joints, lubricate them well with golden oil; then saturate them with white healing energy as you fit them back in place.
5. See all fingers completely healed, all strong and supple once again, then slowly withdraw.
6. Do the same with knee joints, ankles and toes.

(You can use pure sun's rays into the painful area and then paint it blue to soothe it)

9

Sending Light Healing

- Select the person you want to be healed.
- Know the problem of the patient beforehand.
- Sit cross legged in a meditation pose.
- Visualise the white circle over your crown chakra.
- Visualise the white light falling from the circle and covering your full body.
- Visualise yourself as transparent.
- Now softly repeat the person's name you wish to be treated.
- Visualise the person in front of you.
- Visualise a light emanating from your third eye chakra and falling at the problematic area of the person you are treating.
- Visualise the problem being solved.
- Visualise the light covering the person from head to toe.
- Visualise the fingers of his hands and toes taking out dark, oily type of liquid from his body.
- Hold this visualisation till you see clear light passing through.
- Visualise him completely treated.
- Request the person to return back and inform him that he is now completely healed.
- Visualise you are coming back to your original self.
- Visualise the white circle diminishing and vanishing.
- Relax for a few moments before opening your eyes.

It is guaranteed that through this exercise you can treat and cure many of the ailments in a person's body.

10

Visual Meditation Exercise: The Universal Bank

- Do the breathing technique and reach the Alpha level.
- Go to your favourite place of relaxation (your sanctuary).
- Relax for a few minutes — fly if you wish, go visiting your relatives/friends.
- Just relax.
- After you have relaxed, close your eyes and repeat the following words "By the power given to me by my higher self, I wish to go to the Universal Bank".
- Feel yourself travelling.
- Open your eyes (visualise) and you will find yourself in front of a building on which is written "THE UNIVERSAL BANK".
- Climb the steps.
- Start walking towards the doors.
- Do everything at a leisurely pace.
- Push the door inwards
- You come across a single counter, which is being attended by a beautiful female (always visualise the opposite gender).
- See her looking at you and smiling.
- "Good morning, Sir," she says
- Reply in sweet tones, "Good morning to you".
- "Can I help you?" she asks you.
- Repeat the following words, "Yes, I want to withdraw US$1,000,000.00 (or any figure you wish to withdraw)".

- "One minute, sir," she says and opens up a drawer to give you a blank banker's cheque. "Can you fill this in?" she asks.
- Fill in the amount you wish to withdraw. Be confident. Be assured. This is the Universal Bank — you ask and it shall be yours. After filling in the cheque and signing it, hand it over the counter to the lady.
- Visualise her reading and requesting you to hold on.
- Visualise her entering the cabin on the other side of the room.
- Visualise her bringing in a leather suitcase with the cash.
- Visualise her handing over the same to you.
- Visualise you accepting the suitcase with the cash and checking for authenticity.
- Visualise yourself thanking the lady and wishing her a good day and leaving the bank.

Come out of the Universal Bank and thank the bank for making your realisation come true.

Repeat the following words — "By the power given to me by my higher self, I wish to return to my favourite place of relaxation."

Visualise yourself in your favourite place of relaxation.

Come back to your physical self whenever you want to do so.

Part IV

Reiki 2: Day 2

1

Absentee Healing

*O*n this side of the globe, we live far away from our country, from our family, relatives and friends.

The only contact being e-mails (which is rare), postal letters and telephone calls. Of course, we do miss our families and friends.

The only major burden on our shoulder is the 24 hours rattling of the chatter-box mind .... so, how's your family? So, how's your family? So, how's your family? This goes on and on and on and on, till people go berserk.

Can we control this rattling? Yes, if we know the mind control technique we can, but, also, if we think deeply on this question of "So, how's your family?" We can smile and say "in excellent health", the rattling will automatically stop.

But, how do we get that confidence, how do we justify the answer "in excellent health"?

It is simple, from our favourite place of relaxation, we can go to our hometown and as a casual visitation, without touching anything, without speaking we observe everyone and everything, then we quietly return to our favourite place.

During our above visit if we have seen any of our family members/relatives/friends who are not in perfect health, we can treat them from our house or from the favourite place itself.

Here comes the importance of the Absentee Healing technique, which is categorised in two:

(1) The short from of Reiki.
(2) The long form of Reki.

Also, these techniques can be used for healing your friends and colleagues who cannot be reached immediately.

I wish you all good luck and again assure you that these are tried techniques where results have been achieved over and over again.

2

Reiki — Short Form

*O*kay, this is where we start Reiki in a different form. Can any one tell me why the short form of Reiki?

"...."

"Prakash?"

"Maybe, due to the lack of time, this Reiki is taught," said Prakash dubiously.

"Right, you have hit the nail at the first shot. Let's take an example. You are a full-fledged Reiki channel, unlike the ones who have just learnt to give Reiki on the 6 or 12 positions of the body.

"Just think, you are travelling in the bus, and you see a cute little girl, who is crying away to glory, only to find that this baby has a severe toothache. What you cannot do is give her a full Reiki that will take 1 hour 18 minutes. At this time, the short form of Reiki will help.

"Just try to become friendly with the child. Repeat the attitude of gratitude fast, then casually place your hands on the area of pain and start drawing the symbols — the Hon Sha Ze Sho Nen, the Say Hay Ki and the Cho Ku Ray, draw each symbol once and repeat it thrice. Give Reiki in the same position for 10 to 15 minutes.

"Believe me the child will be relieved, but she has to get medical attention fast."

"This was in person. But, what if the person is not there. Someone you know is suffering from some pain in the body, and you know you do not have the time to give a full body treatment, what do you do?

"Yes, you give the Absentee Healing — well, here is what you do."

(1) Say the attitude of gratitude.
(2) Draw first, second and third symbols in your third eye chakra.
(3) Cover yourself in white light.
(4) Visualise the person you want treated, cover him/her in white light.
(5) Draw first, second and third symbols in the patient's third eye chakra.
(6) Draw first, second and third symbols in the patient's heart chakra.
(7) Draw first, second and third symbols in the areas of pain (diseased parts) of the patient.
(8) Keep contact for two to three minutes.
(9) Close the process by drawing first, second and third symbols in your third eye chakra.

3

The Reiki Box

*W*hat's a Reiki box?

I call it the magic box.

This Reiki/magic box has shown me many miracles with many of my students.

"Miracles? Box? I do not understand Sir?"

"Okay, I will try to make you understand."

The story of Vishaal:

It was 9.30 p.m. I was preparing to sleep when the telephone rang. I jerked and picked up the phone. It was from one Mr. Kodikal. "Mr. Mohan, I have your reference from *Gulf News*," he said. "My wife is suffering from chronic arthritis and deformation has started, let us ask you — do you think she can be treated?"

I gulped — chronic arthritis? deformation? I had never taken a case of this serious nature before. I closed my eyes and asked for permission from my higher self, I asked for guidance and asked another question, "How long has she been suffering".

"Eight years" — a simple two-word answer.

"What's her age?" I queried.

"63 years".

"Wow," I muttered under my breath.

"Well?" Mr. Kodikal was waiting for my answer.

"Where do you live, Mr. Kodikal?" I asked.

He replied by giving the location of his house.

"I am coming, now," I said. I kept the phone on the cradle and changed my clothes. Within 20 minutes I was at Mr. Kodikal's house looking at a frail lady in a wheel chair.

I gave her a Reiki session on the spot mixing this with visualisation exercises, leaking out the pain from the knee joints, elbow and wrists. After about 45 minutes, I looked at her. She was smiling. The pain had reduced.

I looked at Mr. Kodikal.

"She will walk," I was confident.

"How long will it take?" he asked.

"I cannot give the period, but your son has to come and learn Reiki from me. I will appoint two of my students who are Reiki masters to give treatment twice daily. You pray, we serve. Leave results to nature."

"Okay," Mr. Kodikal replied, "my son will be coming in for the classes. When are they?"

"Tomorrow," I replied, and added: "What's your son's name?"

"Vishaal".

Anuradha — the lady's name — is now completely cured. She walks around without any support of a human or walking stick. Her chronic arthritis has almost vanished, thanks to two of my most brilliant students — Mr. Narayan and his wife Mrs. Nagratna.

Vishaal has been working very hard at his job. When I taught the Reiki box in the classroom, he refused to accept this foolish method, stating that boxes cannot do miracles. But, then he put in an affirmation in the box which read "I am promoted as a manager" and put in a date.

Now, it so happened, that during that time, a vacancy did arise for the post of a manager, but, as he was too good at his present job, the general manager did not deem fit to take him out of his present job and upgrade him as a manager.

That day Vishaal called me and challenged me that he could never get the job, whatever I did. I insisted that this vacancy had risen just because of the affirmation in the Reiki box and this vacancy was for him. "Don't give up, keep giving Reiki to the box for one more month, believe me, Vishaal, this vacancy is for you — YOU WILL GET PROMOTED."

Vishaal shrugged away. But promised to be a good boy and continue giving Reiki to the Reiki box.

I almost forgot about it, when (I think it was about 21 to 22 days after our meeting) I was cooking when the phone rang. I picked up the phone to hear Vishaal's excited voice.

'Mr. Mohan — I GOT IT!'

'WOW!" I shouted with glee. "You have done it, I told you, this vacancy was for you."

Now, Vishaal is working as a manager, whilst another affirmation is already in the Reiki box for another promotion in the coming 18 months. WILL HE GET IT? Well, it is for you to decide.

"Mr. Makkar, can you tell us what this Reiki box is?" asked Geeta impatiently.

I smiled. It is always the case. AAAAAH — The Reiki box. Well, here it comes.

The Reiki box is nothing but an ordinary soapbox. This can be activated with the following method:

1. Say the complete attitude of gratitude (for attitude and for gratitude, I thank myself for being here, I thank Reiki for being here, I thank the Reiki box for being here).
2. Cover self with white light.
3. Hold the box in both your hands.
4. Give symbols to yourself — (the first, second and third) from third eye.
5. Give symbols to the Reiki box — (the first, second and third) from third eye.
6. See Reiki box covered in white light for about two to three minutes.
7. Close with three symbols — first, second and third — from third eye (this closes self).

Your Reiki box is now activated. Now, you have to put in affirmations in this box.

"What are affirmations?" I put in a general question to the class.

As usual, silence follows.

"An affirmation is an intention which is written in positive, perfect continuous tense i.e., you see a future event as happening here and now". e.g., "Day by day in every way, I am feeling better and better and better".

We have the Reiki box ready; we are now looking for the contents of the Reiki box — which are the affirmations. Here are some of the rules for the Reiki Box.

Contents of Reiki Box

(1) The Reiki box should include only one affirmation on one sheet of paper.

(2) Intentions should be positive, perfect continuous tense, i.e., you see any future event happening here and now.

(3) All intentions should be as positive affirmations.

(4) For depression ask yourself the question "How do I feel?" Write the opposite (e.g., "How do I feel?" "I feel I am not being loved as I should be". Affirmation will be. "I am being loved and respected").

(5) Cleaning of Reiki box is essential as and when the intentions are fulfilled.

(6) Uncleared intentions. If your intentions are not fulfilled on the given date, re-write them with different dates.

(7) Write affirmations that are nearer to your heart and not nearer to your ego.

(8) You can put your own intentions, your friends'/relatives' intentions also.

(9) You can put stamp/passport sized photos for healing in the Reiki box.

(10) Invite friends' intentions in Reiki box or put in positive affirmations and let your friends sign themselves with date of fulfilment.

(11) You need not know all the intentions of the Reiki box.

(12) The Reiki box can be of any material — the best is which appeals to your eyes.

(13) Keep this Reiki box in a clean and safe place (privacy is a must).

(14) Give Reiki to the Reiki box twice daily for approximately two to three minutes each time.

Most of my students claim that many of their dreams have been realised and they are very happy with this technique which is unique.

Try it — it may change your life for the better.

Some of the Affirmations

- I am in perfect health.
- I am financially stable.
- I am prospering every minute.
- I see every negative point with a positive view.
- I love everyone around me.
- I am becoming very patient.
- Those surrounding me are in perfect health.
- My sense of perception is increasing.
- My attitude towards everyone is brotherly.
- I love life in every form.
- Day by day, in every way, I am becoming better and better and better.
- Divine love is guiding me and I am always taken care of.
- Every day I am growing more financially prosperous.
- Everything I need is coming to me easily and effortlessly.
- I always communicate clearly and effectively.
- I am lovable and a loving person.
- I am always in the right place at the right time, successively engaged in the right activity.
- I am an active channel of creative energy.
- I am dynamically self-expressive.
- I am learning to love and accept myself as I am.
- I am now enjoying everything I do.
- I am rich in consciousness and manifestation.
- I am talented, intelligent and creative.

- I am vibrantly healthy and radiantly beautiful.
- I am whole in myself.
- I am true to myself.
- I love myself.
- I am responsible for my own well being.

You can rewrite the above affirmations in your own handwriting and place them in the Reiki box. Moreover, daily reading of the above affirmations can have a hypnotic effect on your subconscious mind, making you a better and more successful person.

4

Reiki — Long Form

*A*s stated earlier, most of the time it is a must that a full form of Reiki has to be given to a person who is not in your presence.

1st Alternative

For this, you have to give the long form of Reiki.

To start with please remember the person you are sending Reiki to is in bed or at least at home. Call the person up and confirm the person is at home. (Reiki seems to make people dizzy at times — unfortunately if the person is driving — complications may arise due to your giving Reiki at that time — as accidents can occur).

This type of long healing is done the same way, as we do the self-healing the only difference being the following words:

First you declare your body to be (the person's name you are treating):

"I declare my body to be Mr. Xxxxxxxx's body.
"I thank myself for being here"
"I thank Reiki for being here"
"I thank Mr. Xxxxxxxx's for being here"

Start, as you would do the self-cleansing technique.

After completing the full Reiki (26 positions) undeclare yourself as follows: "I declare this body to be my own Mr. (your name) body".

2nd Alternative

Give Reiki to your right thigh declaring it to be the patient's front side of the body, and the left thigh to be the back side of the body. We do the exercise as follows:

- Say the attitude of gratitude.
- Draw the first, second and third symbols on your third eye.
- Cover yourself in white light.
- Now imagine the patient whom you are about to give Reiki.
- Cover the patient in white light.
- Draw the first, second and third symbols on the patient's third eye and heart chakras.
- Declare the front portion of your right thigh is (name of the patient) front body.
- Give Reiki to your right thigh as you would give Reiki to any person's front body (all 19 positions).
- Do the spirals — and lock the energy.
- Now, declare the left portion of your thigh to be the patient's back side of the body.
- Cover the seven points.
- Close with chakra balancing.
- Do the stroking.
- Do the caressing.
- Undeclare your thighs as your own.

This completes the complete Absentee Healing Method of Reiki.

5

The Many Faces of Reiki

*R*eiki has other faces also: Like you can heal the struggles in your life, release the tensions that you are going through, loosen the auras in your body (this is very helpful for depression cases), if you are not being healed, Reiki can again help you.

Do not worry if you do not find time to heal, whilst in bed, programme Reiki to be sent to anyone at any time on any given date, you can create future with Reiki, heal the dead if you feel you want to. If you are an introvert and are shy of people, why not try the mental method of healing?

Shall we start?

Healing of Struggles

If you feel you can relax, relax.

Else do the breathing technique — Remember 4 in, 4 hold, 4 out and 4 hold.

You will feel relaxed.

Now, mentally scan your body and see where the pain is accumulating.

Draw the three symbols on that area.

Place your Reiki hands on that area till you feel peaceful.

Healing of Tensions

Relax by the above method and/or breathing technique.

Look at the tension that absorbs much of your time and energy.

Declare the same to your friend whom you trust, if not, write down this tension on a clean sheet of paper.

Give white light to this paper.
Draw the three symbols on this paper.
Visualise the tension being dissolved.

6

Energy Circulation Exercise

*D*uring the 21 days of self-treatment, it is possible that you feel acute pain on your back in the hara/root chakra region or enhanced sexual urge. This is indicative that the Kundalini has been touched and at this stage if you do not want to have sexual intercourse, you can transform this energy to higher consciousness by doing the energy circulation exercise as follows :

1. Lie on your back with your knees raised and feet touching the ground.
2. Feet should be slightly apart with hands at your sides, palms up.
3. Close your eyes.
4. Imagine a black ball (the size of a gold ball) on your genitals.
5. With every ingoing breath tie the ball with the breath.
6. With every outgoing breath pull the ball upward towards our crown chakra, turning the black ball into white.
7. The ball should be thrown out from the crown chakra only at the 36th breath and at this time the ball should be completely white.
8. Should the ball slip back, restart the count.

Good exercising.

7

Practical Exercise:
Absentee Healing

*P*neumonia/wet-cough/asthma (wheezing).

(1) Centralise yourself.
(2) Go to alpha.
(3) Go to your laboratory.
(4) Discuss the case with your counsellors.
(5) Call the patient.
(6) Open the chest area.
(7) See the phlegm/dust on the lungs.
(8) For the phlegm start the draining with two taps on the bottom of each lung. See phlegm has been drained away. For the dust vacuum out the same.
(9) Once the lungs are emptied out, you can start the healing process by visualizing healing body tape covering sore areas and soothing, pain-removing oil being passed through and around all the tubes, (also effective for bronchitis) as well as over the inner lining of the lungs themselves.
(10) Ensure that throat, bronchial tubes and lungs all healed and functioning normally as you give them a final shot of white energy and instruct the inner mind to repeat the procedure at an interval of 12 hours until a relapse is no longer likely.

8

Visual Meditation Exercise: Let's Travel

During the classes held on regular basis, students do not believe that Astral travel is possible.

See friends and relatives and then return with information on what it has seen and heard — HOW CAN THIS BE TRUE? — they ask.

Well, it is simpie.

The physical body that functions is made up of five materials — earth, water, ether, air and fire. Even the Bible says: "Dust thou art and to dust thou shall return."

But what about the ethereal body? What about the soul?

"Thou shall rise after death," says the Bible — "This '*thou*' is the ethereal body, which comes from the word ether and is known also as the twin soul. This twin soul or the ethereal body is attached to the physical body with a golden chord. At the time of death this cord is detached from the body and then the ethereal body in which the chakras and the soul also exist cannot attach itself to the body again.

At this stage, the ethereal body remains in the zone as per their karmas, and the soul, also known as the Blue Pearl, is reborn. One of the few theories explains that this soul is immediately put in the womb of a woman who is in the third month of pregnancy, and, for the next six months this soul, in the mother's womb, is shown the life he/she has led.

The pure nectar of this explanation is the ethereal body and the golden cord attached to it with the physical body. The cord is extendable and, though attached to the physical body, can travel millions of miles — in either direction. These types of travels are also known as astral travels.

During the astral travels you can perform miracles, which will be known only to you. You can visit friends and relatives.

Our purpose of ethereal travel is to detach the ethereal body from the physical body and request it to visit any place we choose.

Here is what we do:

First we go to our favourite place of relaxation.

(1) Relax for some time.

(2) Repeat the following words "By the power given to my higher self, I request my ethereal body to come in front of me."

(3) (Here you may see a grayish/bluish substance in front of you — at this stage you will be unable to move any of your body parts, clinically you may be dead at this time, the pulse rate may have dropped to 3 to 5 beats/second).

(4) When you see your ethereal body in front of you, request this body to visit any of your relatives, friends any one you wish.

(5) Within seconds you will feel you are there — in the house you wished to be.

(6) (Two things are very important here — 1. Try to see the calendar in that house and 2. make a mental note of date and time).

(7) Take a note of all surroundings. You will be unable to touch anything. Everything you see may be opposite of what you may have seen in the physical body. For example, when you are facing the kitchen the bathroom door may be on the right-hand side (physical), but in the astral level the bathroom door will appear on the left-hand side. See the

bedsheets, the table covers, the mats, cutlery, people, their clothes, colours on the walls every possible detail you can gather.

(8) Request your ethereal body to come back to your physical body. It should be back within seconds.

(9) Be careful not to get up immediately.

(10) Lie down still, relaxed.

(11) After a few minutes, slowly open your eyes and assess how you are feeling. If you are feeling fresh, get up, if not, close your eyes again and relax for a few more minutes, it may be due to the ethereal body not coming back to the physical body completely.

(12) When you are up and about, try to recollect what had happened and what you had seen. Jot everything down. Do not rely on your memory. These thoughts sooner or later disappear.

(13) Write a letter to the person whose house you have visited giving descriptions, be vague and brief, just say you had a dream and you saw....

(14) Do not be surprised if your friend answers what you saw was 100 per cent correct.

9

Visual Meditation Exercise: Activating Your Ethereal Body

- Sit/lie down in a comfortable position.
- Take a deep breath to the count of 4 filling in your breath to the navel. Stop your breath to the count of 4. Breathe out to the count of 4 from your mouth.
- Repeat till you feel completely relaxed.
- Visualise a white circle over your crown chakra.
- Bring this white circle towards your root chakra from the spinal column.
- See the white circle being attached to your root chakra.
- See the root chakra rotating and emanating red light.
- Move the white circle to the sexual chakra and attach the same to it.
- See the sexual chakra rotating and see an orange light flow out of the chakra.
- Move the white circle to the solar plexus chakra and attach the same to it.
- See the solar plexus chakra rotating and throwing out pale yellow light.
- Now, move this white circle to your heart chakra and attach it.
- See the heart chakra rotating and green light splash in circles.
- Move the white circle to your throat chakra and attach it.
- See the throat chakra rotating. See a light blue light coming out of the throat chakra.

- Move the white circle to your third eye chakra and attach the same to it.
- See the third eye chakra rotating and emanating an indigo light.
- Bring the white circle of light to the crown chakra. Attach this white circle to the crown chakra and see the crown chakra activated. See a violet light emerge from the crown chakra.
- Bring the white circle to your front side and attach it to the third eye chakra. See the third eye chakra rotating and give out an indigo coloured light.
- Slip this white circle into your mouth and from over the soft spot above the tongue into the throat chakra. Attach this circle to your throat chakra. See the throat chakra rotating and giving out a light blue light.
- Bring down the white circle to your heart chakra. Attach the white circle to the heart chakra. Visualise the heart chakra giving out green light.
- Bring the white circle down to the solar plexus chakra. Repeat above and visualise the solar plexus chakra give out a light yellow light.
- Bring the white circle down to your sexual chakra. Repeat above. Visualise orange colour light come out from the sexual chakra.
- Bring the white circle to the centre of your root chakra. See the white light evaporate.
- Now, see all the chakras rotating from the root chakra to the crown chakra from your spinal column and from the crown chakra to your root chakra from the front side of your body. You will see only a white colour light emanating at a very high speed.
- Increase the speed. As you increase the speed you will see another body that is attached to your physical body starts to move. Move this body which is also of white/greyish colour to your left and right side.
- Move this ethereal body in front of you. You can see yourself now. Let this ethereal body float to the roof. See yourself lying down.

- Slowly, let the ethereal body come back to your body and settle down properly.
- Visualise the white circle slow up its speed and finally stop.
- Put both your palms on your eyes.
- Open your eyes under your palms.
- Relax and open your eyes.

10

The Yin and the Yang:
The Pain Killers

*T*his is a unique technique yet a simple one.

How did I come across it?

Well, one day, it so happened that I was reading a book. In this book, I came across the following story of a sage, a sufi, a saint.

It so happened that this saint was travelling by a train with his disciples. When the train stopped at a particular station, an old man saw this saint and invited him for dinner.

This old man was so poor that many a time he found it difficult even to feed himself. But, somehow, the saint accepted the invitation much to the annoyance of his disciples.

After having the meal at the old man's home, the saint saw that the young girl, who served him, was full of white marks on the body.

Now, the saint wanted to return and continue the journey, but not before repaying the old man for all the love he got from him.

So, he took the girl's hands in his hands, and lo and behold! the saint was full of white marks, but the girl had become completely clean. She had turned into a very beautiful maiden.

The disciples were perplexed. But, quietly the saint went out of the house, and, sat under a birch tree, and, again the disciples saw a miracle, the birch tree took the white marks on it and the saint was cleared of the white marks (Rune Power?) And after a few minutes the tree itself was free from the white marks.

143

After reading this story, I pondered for weeks over this. Whilst sleeping at night, I requested my higher self to take me to the place as a silent witness to see what had happened in that village.

In the morning when I woke up, I had pieces of images in my thoughts. That day, a very fat lady walked into my house for treatment. She had problems with her left elbow joint, which pained very severely.

A thought rose in my mind: why not try this method of the saint?

I took her hands in my hand and told her what to do; giving her the "click" point that would indicate the pain had vanished.

I was thrilled when just after three minutes the "click" came.

I looked at her and smiled. "Yes", she was puzzled. The pain had gone. What happened?

Here's the conversation after the click:

"What happened?"

"My pain's gone"

"Completely?"

"Yes" — there was still disbelief in her voice.

"Since when did you have this pain?"

"Last three years" — pause, then "I have consulted many doctors, ayurvedic and homeopaths, but, there has been no relief."

"Who referred you to me?"

"Your student Bhavna," she replied.

I assured her that the pain would not return, and, if it does, please return.

She has never come back.

But, three hours later, after the above treatment, I felt a severe pain in my left elbow. I ignored this pain, not knowing what it was.

Then two hours later, the pain became unbearable. I found tears rolling out of my eyes. What happened? I started recollecting my thoughts and found out that I had taken the pain away from that lady's elbow.

Suddenly, IT HIT ME! Yes, I had taken the pain away from the lady, but what had I done with it. PUT IT IN MY BODY. So, the pain was still in my body. But I had never let it out.

Immediately I sat in a meditation pose and after 15 minutes of meditation, I found complete relief in my left elbow.

From that day onwards, I have treated dozens of cases, where immediate relief is required with this technique, which I have named "the Yin and the Yang".

One more case I treated with this technique was of Mahesh. During the weekend my family and a few friends were travelling in a car to attend a party. One of the occupants in the car was Mahesh. I could see his eyes were reddish and a friend of his (Prakash) was puffing into a handkerchief and putting that on his eyes.

On reaching the house (a studio apartment), I saw Mahesh's eyes were completely red. I instantly knew it was conjunctivitis. I took Mahesh to the kitchen and kept my hands on his eyes. After a few minutes when I removed the hands, his eyes had cleared. The time was 12.15 a.m.

I did not have the place to throw away that diseased energy, so I withheld it in me, for had I taken it away from me, it would be possible it could have gone to someone in that single room apartment. By 3.00 a.m. my eyes had gone completely red.

The guests in the house were shocked. They knew Mahesh had conjuctivitis, but suddenly he was cleared of it and I had the same problem in me now. Mahesh explained that I had done something. They could not comprehend what had happened.

By 4.00 a.m. when we left the house, my eyes were watering profusely. My wife had to drive us back home. Once at home, I sat in the meditation pose and within 30 minutes of meditation, my eyes had cleared and I was perfect again.

At 10.00 a.m. most of the guests came to visit me for they knew that I must be in tremendous pain. Again they were in for a shock. I was up and about and smiling.

They requested I should teach them this technique which of course I refused.

My question to them was this:

Do you have enough love in you to take other people's pain in your body and suffer yourself? Remember, everytime the pain cannot be washed away, some of it will always remain with you. Are you willing to suffer for others? Yes, Christ did, but, will you?"

If yes, go ahead and go to the next chapter.

11

The Yin and the Yang: Method of Healing

*T*his treatment is based on the fact that pain is always black in colour. This pain can be either hard like a rock (chronic pain), soft like a jelly (acute pain), or similar to cotton.

What we have to do is, hit this pain with a white light that goes from our right hand to the patient's left hand. This light travels at a very high speed hitting the black pain and smashing it, crushing it or melting it, which then travels through the patient's right hand and is then thrown into your left hand which you retain it in yourself.

You have to indicate to the patient the following:

(1) He visualises a white light falling from your right hand into his left hand.
(2) Imagine this light travelling towards his shoulders and towards his right hand.
(3) Hitting the pain and melting/breaking the pain into small sandlike pieces.
(4) The pain which is black in colour passing with the force of white light into your left hand.
(5) Till the patient does not feel the white light fluently passing from his left hand to his right hand he will continue visualising the white light hitting the black pain and the black pain giving way.

(6) When the white light passes from his left to right hand, he has to press his left-hand thumb on your left hand, indicating the session is over.

(7) Wait for a few seconds and release the hands that are clasped.

The pain is now in your hand, and, the patient is relieved. What you have to do is this:

(1) Sit in a meditation pose.

(2) Visualise a white/golden/electrical violet light circle on your crown chakra.

(3) See this light circle spinning — fast, faster, faster, faster — as it is spinning it is emitting the colour that is being poured over your crown chakra and into your third eye chakra.

(4) As you visualise see this light passing from your third eye chakra to your throat, heart, solar plexus, hara, sexual and root chakras.

(5) Visualise this light energy pass through your shoulder blades into your arms, elbows and thrust that black pain into your palms.

(6) Visualise the black pain seeping out of your hands till a clear light does not pass through.

(7) The balance energy will cover, protect and energise you keeping you completely fit.

Thank the energy for the miraculous healing.

12

Summary

*C*ongratulations! You have now completed the Reiki 2 course.
Let's summarise what we have learnt in Reiki 2 — first, we
shall segregate the mind control and Reiki sessions:
In Reiki we have learnt:

(1) The symbols and their meanings. Also, we have learnt how
many sets of symbols are to be drawn on each position.
(2) We have learnt the absentee healing method — where it is a
must, ensure that the person you are healing is at home when
the healing is being sent.
(3) We have also learnt the short form of Reiki — which works
miracles in a short duration — for this too it is requested to
ensure that the person you are healing is at home when the
healing is being sent.
(4) The magic box — officially named "the Reiki box". You have
to be very careful to ensure that the affirmations written by
you are as taught to you in this chapter.
(5) The long form of Reiki is a technique where you declare your
'body' or 'your thighs' (left and right) to be the person you
are healing, and you have to give full Reiki inclusive of the
spiralling, chakra balancing, stroking and caressing, after
which you have to declare your body or your thighs to be your
own.
(6) In the many faces of Reiki we have learnt different uses of
Reiki.

In Visual Meditation we have learnt:

(1) Sending healing light.

(2) The Universal Bank — the more you practise on this, the clearer your visualisation, the better chances will occur for realising your dreams.

(3) In Let's Travel, continuous practice of this exercise sets about your ethereal body to travel in different zones. But, do ensure that the telephone/s are kept off the hook, the mobiles and pages are switched off and doubly ensure that you are not disturbed when you do this exercise.

(4) In activating your ethereal body we learnt how to loosen the auras and how to travel. We have to take all the precautions of No. 3 — 'Let's Travel' exercise.

We have also learnt the sound meditation and the Yin and the Yang painkillers. Please do not practise the Yin and the Yang if you are sick or suffering from body aches. Also do ensure that immediately as the pain is taken out of the patient's body, you sit in meditation yourself and do the exercise taught in this chapter till you get full relief from the pain in your body.

13

It's Time for an Examination

QUESTION PAPER

Another wonder achieved. Patience is always rewarded. How do you feel on completing the Reiki 2 course? Elated? Excited? Let's see how you fare in this small examination:

(1) Can you draw all the three symbols and write their meanings?
(2) What are the absentee healing methods?
(3) Write any 10 affirmations from your Reiki box.
(4) What are the different uses of Reiki?
(5) How do you activate your ethereal body?
(6) Have you submitted your questions for Reiki 1?
(7) Who gave you the Reiki 2 attunement?
(8) What were your experiences?

A REIKI 2 CERTIFCATE will be issued to you if you can answer the above questions and post it to:

Mohan Makkar
c/o UBS Publishers' Distributors Ltd.
5 Ansari Road, Darya Ganj,
New Delhi-110 002 (India)

Please ensure the certificate is duly filled in to suit your requirements.

The REIKI 2 CERTIFICATE will be posted to you in 45 days' time if the questions are found to have been answered satisfactorily. If the questions have not been answered satisfactorily, we shall advise you accordingly.

You will also be complemented with the Reiki 3A Attunement Booklet, which will take you to the level of Reiki master.

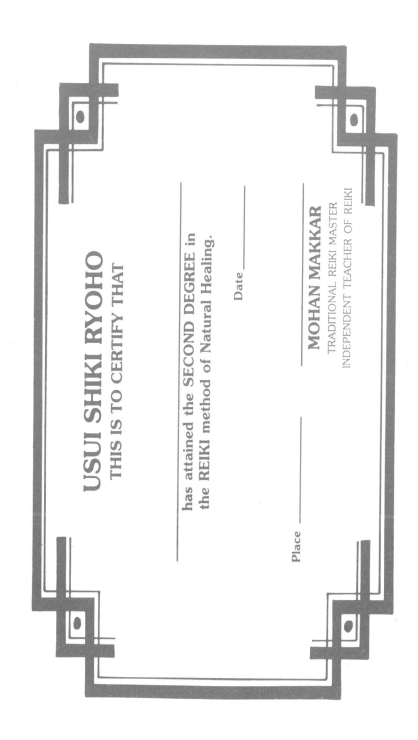

USUI SHIKI RYOHO

THIS IS TO CERTIFY THAT

_____

has attained the SECOND DEGREE in the REIKI method of Natural Healing.

Date _____

Place _____

MOHAN MAKKAR
TRADITIONAL REIKI MASTER
INDEPENDENT TEACHER OF REIKI

Part V

Reiki 3A

1

A Discussion

*W*elcome to the Master's degree class.

We have achieved some direction in our life. Our life is a log floating in a stream with no direction. Wherever our life takes us we go. Our life is like a wild horse. No controls — like a car without a steering wheel.

Now, we have the steering wheel — Reiki.

We have taken the control of our wheel — the reins are in our hands and the wild horse has been broken. We are sitting on the log that was floating aimlessly down the stream — all in all we have DIRECTION.

We are one of the few people in the world.

By doing this course, we shall become stronger.

Before that we have to assess what we have learnt.

- We have learnt Reiki — through which we can cure people with the universal energy by our hands.
- In Reiki we have learnt the short form and the long form of Reiki.
- We have learnt the Reiki box where we put in our affirmations.
- Most important — we have learnt to travel in any part of the world, visit anybody at any given time.
- We have our own favourite place of relaxation.
- We have our own laboratory for treatment and our own counsellors.
- We have learnt in part the technique of metaphysical healing.

- We have learnt in part the technique of mind control healing.
- We have learnt to meditate.
- AGAIN, MOST IMPORTANT — we have learnt to use the white light to heal people, circumstances and relations.
- We have learnt the three symbols that made our world of Reiki more powerful.

Now, today we shall increase this power — we shall become Masters — THE REIKI MASTERS.

Now, an illuminating small story of two Tibetan monks.

These monks live a solitary life. They are not allowed to talk, beg, come in contact with the opposite sex etc. etc. etc.

One day as these two monks were travelling they came upon a stream which had to be crossed. The flow of the water was very strong. They saw a young girl, trying to step into the water, but, every time she tried to put her foot in, she stepped back, for fear of being washed away in the stream.

One of the monks just whisked her on his shoulders, stepped into the water and left her on the other side of the stream. The other monk was quiet. Both the monks had travelled a few miles when suddenly the other monk spat out: "But why did you carry her?"

The first monk smiled at his mate and said: "I carried her, I left her — that was it. But, you are still carrying her."

This is what our life is. We are carrying too many corpses on our shoulders. We have so many things in our life that we DO NOT WANT, and, the better part of our life is wasted dwelling in the "NO ZONE."

We dwell on the don'ts and not the do's and lose our focus, as the following story illustrates.

I recollected one more episode of a guy who went para sailing. It was the first time he had jumped from the cliff, and he was doing beautifully well when suddenly the instructor below shouted — "Hey, you see that red car, don't go and bash in there."

That guy's attention was divided. He began searching for the red car below him. He saw the car and, of course, he crashed into the car!

2

What Is Reiki 3A?

L ike the other Reiki sessions, this session is important. It is also unique. It will change you to a better person, more understanding, more loving, and more caring.

Reiki 3 — discussions with the master/teacher brings you to a higher level of understanding the people around you. If someone comes to you, do not shoo that person away. DO NOT JUMP TO CONCLUSIONS.

Sometimes what the ears hear may not be the truth. Also, sometimes what the eyes see is ALSO NOT THE TRUTH.

Do not carry corpses on your shoulders. Let bygones be bygones.

The Master Symbol (see following page) is:

This is drawn from the third eye chakra on the area of the patient's body where the problem exists.

This is a very very powerful symbol and brings results very quickly. Do not go on flaunting this symbol. Be serious in this area of treating people as you will be seeing too many people being healed and also a ratio of people being passed on to the land of no return.

I can just wish you good luck.

3

The Master Symbol

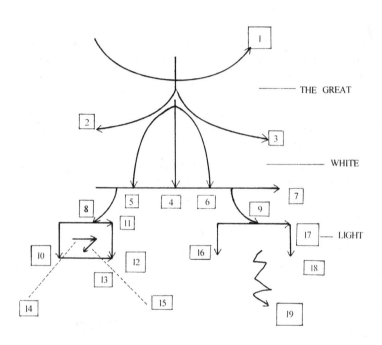

DAI THE GREAT	KU WHITE	MYO LIGHT

4

Do You Need Regression?

*W*hat is regression?

Regression means "progressive decline"

It is not necessary for everyone to undergo a regression or re-birthing course.

You have to take into consideration each of the following:

1. Your relationship with your family members.
2. Your relationship with your friends/colleagues.
3. Your relationship with yourself.
4. Your relationship with your work.
5. Your relationship with each and every aspect of your life.

What we have to ask ourselves is:

Why is our relationship bad with one member of the family and good with the other member? Though you may consider you are very soft spoken and of a very mild nature where others are concerned.

Then why the difference?

Have you ever thought, sometimes, you see a person whom you have never met before, and, instantly you have a bad taste in your mouth? Have you ever asked the question to yourself — Why do I feel this bad taste in my mouth? Why do I feel this hatred in me, I have never seen this person in my life before?

On the other hand, you see a person for the first time, and bingo. You are in love with that person. Again, why?

159

Mainly, on the subject of regression, we take our present status. How is my relationship with my family members, bad? How is their relationship with me, good? If it is good, then something must be wrong with me. It is my fault.

Regression/re-birthing are techniques which slowly and gradually take you into the past making you meet people and enabling you to see events wherein you have suffered and which has affected your present life.

Slowly, the teacher takes you backwards to your childhood and still more to your previous birth. Here you see your life, see the faces of the people and come back to the present life and recognise those faces. Then you make connections. All the way to the past and present, past and again to the present again and again and again. Till you know the relationship the reasons.

The teacher explains and asks you to pardon those people who have harmed you. For, if you do not, you get them back into your next birth. By pardoning them, you complete your relationship with these people, paving a way for them to get out of your life never to return again.

So, if you think that you love someone, and, still it is not working out, go for the regression/re-birthing and maybe YOU WILL HAVE YOUR ANSWER — you never know.

5

Do You Live by the Attitude of Gratitude Way of Life

*L*et me ask you one question? Do not get fidgety, it won't embarrass you.

How may times in a day do you use the "F" word? or say "shit!"

I believe it is most common to do so, say "umpteen" times a day?

What is important to note is that when you say "s-h-i-t" all the emphasis is laid on the sound "SH" which takes out all the pressure from your head.

Similarly the "F" (pronounced Fuh).

This air which is let out in a short outbound breath relieves you immediately and makes you feel comfortable. Most of the time, you may notice that after using such vulgar, dirty words, which are the most in-things, especially amongst the teenagers, you feel relaxed.

So, it is not "shit" which is important. The word can also be "ship" because the emphasis is still the same "SH". Try it sometimes. You will achieve the same results and people around you may not catch on the word for a few days.

Similarly the "F" word should be changed to something like "Fut" instead of "F…" (Fut means 'future')

Such other obscene words can be changed to words that have good meanings.

The exercise is simple, the implementation is hard — but not impossible.

This will take you to a state of attitude of gratitude.

Whilst on the subject of attitude of gratitude, let me ask you another question. No, do not groan. Every question I ask you will take you a step closer to making you a better person, a healthier person, physically, mentally and spiritually.

How many minutes a day do you give to yourself?

The answers I get from my students are not even a single minute.

How may minutes has nature given you in a day? Did you consider that?

Twenty-four hours/day x 60 minutes/hour = 1,440 minutes/day.

Out of these 1440 minutes/day how may times do we thank ourselves for the facilities available to us.

How often do we use, or even feel the word 'thank you'?

Saying thank you to each and every part of our body for working 24 hours of the day non-stop in order to keep us healthy and active.

- The sink in the kitchen for making our task easier by allowing us to wash the utensils on the spot.
- The gas cooker.
- The TV set.
- The sofa set.
- The dining table
- The computer.
- Our family members for making us feeling important.
- Our boss for giving us a job, which feeds our family.

The list is endless, it can go on and on and on.

This acceptance of gratitude will make you humble. Do not ever doubt that nature, the body, the people, the things are not listening. They listen. They act. Everything, anything is ENERGY. You too are ENERGY. From energy to energy thank it. Say, "Thank you for.... " and mean it.

Life will become easier. You will become a different person. You will notice the changes that will come over you ever so slowly.

The armour of irritation will melt away and the ego will vaporise.

Peace will be your forte. Perfect health will smile at you as long as you are in this world.

Accept the problems, solve them, but always "the attitude of gratitude" should be there to make our life one long happy journey.

6

Questions and Answers

I sincerely hope that you have completed the 3A course before answering these questions and do not refer to the notes again.

Once more, before answering these questions, ask yourself, "Have I done the 90 days' cleansing?" If the answer is "yes" go ahead and attempt the questions. If the answer is "no" complete the self-cleansing first, then attempt the questions.

Remember, though I may not see you, I am with you and your answer will give me an insight into your experiences with Reiki. These are enough for me to know, if you are being honest with me.

Now, the questions:

(1) After you finished the Reiki 3A course, you did the 90 days' self-cleansing with the master symbol. What were your experiences?

(2) How do you feel after completing this course?

(3) What do you think of yourself as a whole person? Do you feel you have any more drawbacks in your life?

(4) Write about your drawbacks. I may be able to help you become one with yourself.

(5) Remember, while giving Reiki to others at the 3A level, which is also known as the master level, your motto should be: "Let me lead you gently back to yourself." Why do you think this motto has been chosen.

(6) When it is said "Let me lead you gently back to yourself" what comes to your mind?

(7) How many people have you treated till date? Please write in full the names, their illnesses, period of cure and if the results were positive.

(8) What are your thoughts when you are treating people?

(9) Do you charge fees from the people you are treating?

(10) Do you live by the "attitude of gratitude"?

If your answers and experiences are found to be correct, you will be awarded a Reiki Master's Certificate that will be complementary from myself. Just ask yourself once, "A master is disciplined, a master is unique, a master is patient, understanding and love incarnate, am I so?" If yes, write to me and you shall have the certificate by post within the next 45 days.

This is my attitude for gratitude for doing the course with patience, love and understanding.

Good luck.

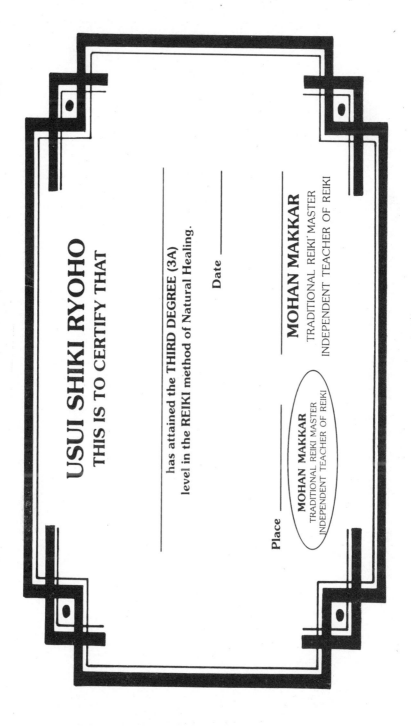

USUI SHIKI RYOHO

THIS IS TO CERTIFY THAT

_____

has attained the THIRD DEGREE (3A)
level in the REIKI method of Natural Healing.

Date _____

Place _____

MOHAN MAKKAR
TRADITIONAL REIKI MASTER
INDEPENDENT TEACHER OF REIKI

MOHAN MAKKAR
TRADITIONAL REIKI' MASTER
INDEPENDENT TEACHER OF REIKI

Part VI

Reiki 3B

1

Preparing for an Attunement

*I*n order to improve the results you receive during the attunement, a process of purification is recommended. This will allow the attunement energies to work more efficiently and create greater benefits for you. The following steps are a must if you need to prove yourself as the best student and achieve maximum results. Follow them if you wish:

(1) Avoid non-vegetarian food for three days prior to attending the classes. These foods often contain drugs in the form of penicillin and female hormones and toxins in the form of pesticides and heavy metals that make your system sluggish and throw it out of balance.

(2) Consider a water or juice fast for one to three days specially if you already are a vegetarian or have experience with fasting.

(3) Minimise your use of coffee and caffeine drinks, else stop completely. These create imbalances in the nervous and endocrine systems. Use no caffeine drinks on the day of the attunement.

(4) Use no alcohol for at least three days prior to the attunement.

(5) Minimise or stop using sweets. Do not eat any chocolates.

(6) Cut down on smoking or do not smoke the day you are attending the classes.

(7) Meditate an hour a day for at least two weeks using the easiest meditation technique, else speak as little as possible.

(8) Reduce or eliminate time watching TV, listening to radio and reading newspapers.

(9) Using time saved for quiet walks, spending time with nature and getting moderate exercises.

(10) Give more attention to subtle impressions and sensations within and around; contemplate their meaning.

(11) Release all anger, fear, jealousy, hate, worry, etc. Create a sacred space within and around you.

(12) Use you Reiki guide (Your Reiki teacher will guide you).

The Technique

Fig - 1

i) Bring Reiki student into the room.

ii) Make the student sit as shown in the photo above.

P.S. Note Gap between the feet.

Fig - 2

i) Stand opposite the student.

ii) If the student has not folded hands instruct as follows:

    a) Please fold your hands, be comfortable.

    b) Close your eyes, do not open your eyes till I tell you to do so.

    c) Thank you.

Fig - 3

i)   Go on your haunches (toes inwards)
ii) Repeat mentally the following:
   (a) I thank myself for being here.
        I request my personality to step
        aside.
   (b) Continue repeating menally "I
        think Dr. Usui for being here.
        I thank Dr. Hayashi for being
        here. I thank Mrs. Takata for
        being here. I thank Mr. Makkar
        for being here. I thank (*insert all
        your family members' names
        here*).
   (c) I thank my Soul leaders for being
        here.
   (d) I request my physical self to step
        aside (*visualize your physical
        self stepping aside*).
   (e) I surrender and let go.

Fig - 4

i)   Half rise yourself. Repeat mentally
     "I thank you for being here. I ask
     your personality to step aside. I ask
     your higher self to be in contact with
     my higher self.   Thank you. (*here
     you have to sense the vibrations in
     your body while watching the 3rd
     Eye Chakra*).

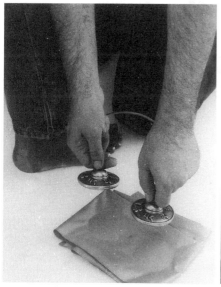

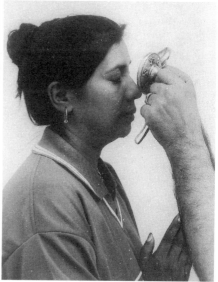

Fig - 5

Fig - 6

Sit on your haunches and pick up the cymbals lying on a mat on your right hand side next to the stool in front.

i) Stretch your hands. Place cymbals nearer to the 3rd Eye Chakra of the student.

ii) Strike cymbals thrice waiting each time for the vibrations to finish.

(**Note**: *When you strike the cymbals in the 3rd Eye Chakra you have to put the cymbals to the ears (Right & Left) till vibrations are over.*)

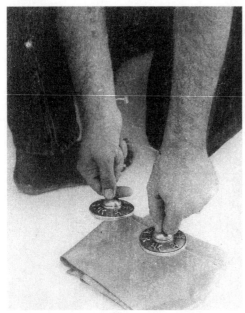

Place cymbals on the mat.

Fig - 7

Stand up in front of the student.

Fig - 8

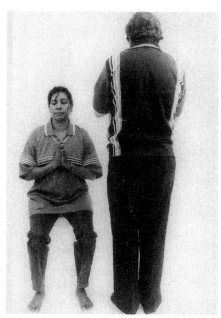

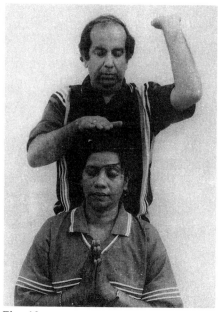

Fig - 9

Step on your Right hand side and mentally
say "Thank you".

Fig - 10

i)   Place your Right hand approx.
3" above the student's 3rd Eye Chakra
and left hand palm upwards, point
towards the sky.

ii) Mentally feel the Reiki energy pass
from your left hand to your right hand
and on to the Crown Chakra of the
student.

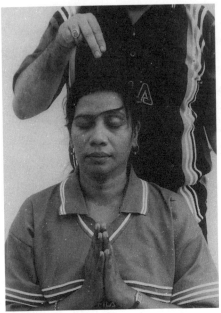

Fig - 11

i)   Draw 'Dai Ku Myo'. Repeat thrice.
ii) Draw 'Cho Ku Ray'. Repeat thrice.
iii) Draw 'Hon sha Ze Sho Nain'. Repeat thrice.
iv) Draw 'Say Hai Ki'. Repeat thrice.

Note: Symbols are to be drawn once and repeated thrice.

Fig - 12

Step on the Right hand side and mentally repeat "Thank you".

i) Come in front of the student.
ii) Place your Right foot between the student's feet.

Fig - 13

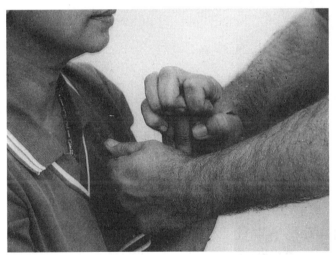

Fig - 14

i) Slightly bend and cover student's nails with your right hand.
Note: Your left hand thumb covers both the thumbs of the student.

ii) Pressurize the fingers and thumbs, whilst drawing "Dai Ku Myo". "Hon sha Ze Sho Nain", "Say Hay Ki" and "Cho Ku Ray" on the 3rd Eye Chakra.

iii) Release hands to catch wrist.
This is known as 'THE SMALL CUP'

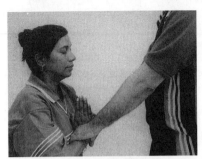

Catch wrists with your hands as above.

Fig - 15

Raise student's hands and blow "Cho" on the Heart Chakra.

Fig - 16

Raise hands again and blow "Ku" on Throat Chakra.

Fig - 17

Raise hands all the way up and blow "Ray" on 3rd Eye Chakra, whilst bringing student's hands on his Crown Chakra. (The breath of "Ray" should pass between the palms of the student).

Fig - 18

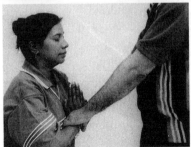

Place hands back on student's Heart Chakra.

Fig - 19

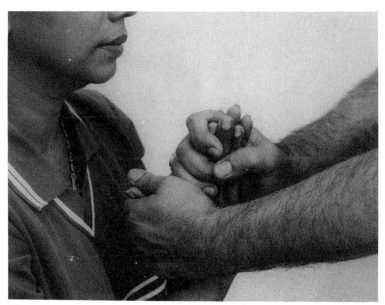

Fig - 20

i)   Cover both the hands of the student with your right hand.
ii) Your left thumb covers both the thumbs of the student.
iii) While pressing all the above draw "Dai Ku Myo", "Hon Sha Ze
     Sho Nain", "Say Hay Ki", "Cho Ku Ray".
iv) Release hands to catch the wrists.
This is known as "The Big Cup".

Fig - 22

Raise student's hands and blow 'Cho' on the Heart Chakra.

Fig - 21

Catch wrists with your hands as above.

Raise hands again and blow 'Ku' on the Throat Chakra.

Fig - 23

Raise hands all the way up and blow "Ray" on 3rd Eye Chakra, whilst bringing student's hands on his Crown Chakra. (The breath of "Ray" should pass between the palms of the student).

Fig - 24

Student is in this position after blowing of "Cho Ku Ray".

Fig - 25

Step on your right side and mentally say "Thank You".

Fig - 26

Draw "Cho Ku Ray". Repeat thrice.

Fig - 27

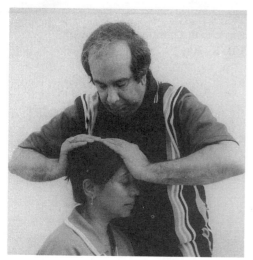

Fig - 28

This is an Attunement

Do as above — pressing slightly. (This is supposed to open the 3rd
Eye Chakra) whilst drawing "Dai Ky Myo", "Hon Sha Ze sho Nain",
"Say Hay Ki", "Cho Ku Ray" once each and repeating thrice.

Fig - 29
Step on RHS.

Fig - 30
Come in front of the student.

Fig - 31

i) Come in front of the student.
ii) Place your right foot between the student's feet.

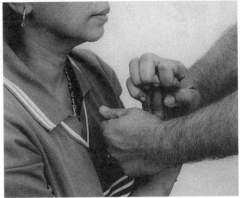

Fig - 32

i) Slightly bend and cover student's nails with your right hand.
   Note: Your left hand thumb covers both the thumbs of the student.

ii) Pressurize the fingers and thumbs, whilst drawing "Dai Ku Myo". "Hon sha Ze Sho Nain", "Say Hay Ki" and "Cho Ku Ray" on the 3rd Eye Chakra.

iii) Release hands to catch wrist.
   This is known as 'THE SMALL CUP'

Fig - 33

Catch wrist with your hands.

Fig - 34

Raise student's hand and blow 'Cho' on the Heart Chakra.'

Raise hands again and blow 'Ku' on the Throat Chakra.

Fig - 35

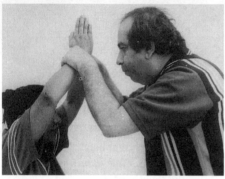

Raise hands all the way up and blow "Ray" on 3rd Eye Chakra, whilst bringing student's hands on his Crown Chakra. (The breath of "Ray" should pass between the palms of the student).

Fig - 36

Place student's hands on the Heart Chakra.

Fig - 37

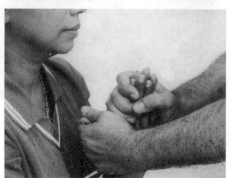

i)   Cover both the hands of the student with your right hand.
ii) Your left thumb covers both the thumbs of the student.
iii) While pressing all the above draw "Dai Ku Myo", "Hon Sha Ze Sho Nain", "Say Hay Ki", "Cho Ku Ray".
iv) Release hands to catch the wrists.
     This is known as "The Big Cup".

Fig - 38

Fig - 39
Catch wrists with your hands as above.

Fig - 40

Raise student's hands and blow 'Cho' on the Heart Chakra.

Raise hands again and blow 'Ku' on Throat Chakra.

Fig - 41

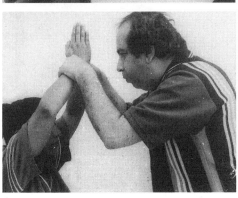

Raise hands all the way up and blow "Ray" on 3rd Eye Chakra, whilst bringing student's hands on his Crown Chakra. (The breath of "Ray" should pass between the palms of the student).

Fig - 42

Fig - 43

Student is in this position after blowing of "Cho Ku Ray".

Fig - 44

Place hands as above on Heart Chakra.

Fig - 45

Step on your right side and mentally say "Thank You".

Fig - 46

Draw "Cho Ku Ray".
Repeat thrice.

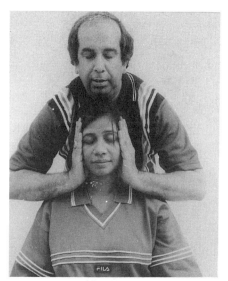

Fig - 47a

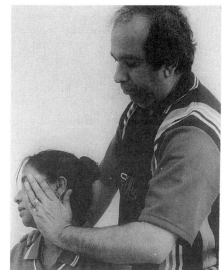

Fig - 47b

This is an Attunement

(i) Both hands covering face (Fig. 47-a) whilst your thumbs rest on the back side of the skull — behind the ear.

(ii) Slightly raise the hand upwards drawing "Dai Ku Myo", "Hon Sha Ze Sho Nain", "Say Hay Ki", "Cho Ku Ray" once and repeating thrice.

Fig - 48
Step on the Right Hand Side,
mentally say "Thank You".

Fig - 49
Stand in front of the student.

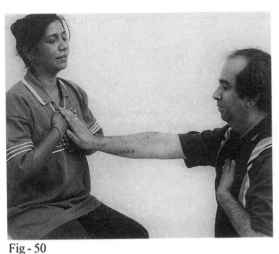

Fig - 50
Go on your haunches.

  (i)   Place your RH on student's hands.
  (ii) Place your LH on your Heart Chakra.
  (iii) Draw "Cho Ku Ray" once repeating thrice.

Fig - 51
Stand up. Step to your RHS.
Softly say : "Come back to
the room. Now you can
open your eyes.   Thank
You."

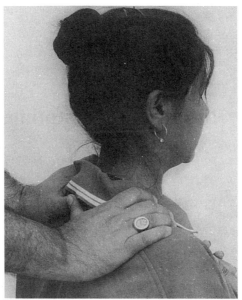

Fig - 52

This is an Attunement

Note: This is the 2nd Day attunement which is same as day-1 attunement. All Figures 1 to 46 are to be done but Fig. 47a & 47b are to be replaced by Fig. 52.

Description:

(i) Your palms lie on the backside of the student's shoulders.

(ii) Your RH thumb covers the LH thumb (covers the 7th vertebra). Pressurize slightly drawing "Dai Ku Myo", "Hon Sha Ze Sho Nain", "Say Hay KI", "Cho Ku Ray".

3

20-minute Meditation

*T*his is what we do. We say we do not want this, and do a hundred things to avoid not wanting that. But, if we turn our thinking and attitude and say "I want this" and create a desire to get that, and do a hundred things to get that, we WILL GET WHAT WE WANT.

Because, our attention is not divided. From negative thoughts we are turning our energy to positive thoughts.

When people visit me, they claim they have diseases, which cannot be healed by doctors. I tell them with confidence: "You will be cured, I promise you." Then, I immediately encircle them in white light and float them into the air.

Be it high or low blood pressure, be it diabetes, asthma, arthritis, rheumatism or any disease that may take months/years to cure. If you do the healing with compassion, love, patience and honesty, the results will follow quickly.

I repeat again what I have repeated before and will repeat again, "Do lots and lots of visualisation exercises, the clearer the picture, the faster the healing will be."

Now, let's do a 20-minute meditation.

This will be a simple meditation with the following steps:

(1) Sit in your favourite comfortable position or lie down comfortably.
(2) Close your eyes.
(3) Follow your breath going in and coming out.
(4) Follow your breath and listen to the breathing sound.

(5) Continue doing the same.
(6) While following your breath, listen to your heart beats.
(7) Continue doing this for the rest of the time.

Open your eyes slowly.
Do these exercises two to three times a day.

4

What We Have Learnt So Far

A SUMMARY

I know in the midst of the lesson I have stopped. Remember that this is Teacher's degree. We have to go very slow — yes, at a snail's pace. Move like the tortoise. Safe and sure.

Before we proceed further, we have to ensure the following:

(1) We have mastered all the Reiki positions.

(2) The attunement techniques for Reiki 1 x 2 days, Reiki 2 and Reiki 3A are learnt by heart. We have the mat and the cymbals ready in the attunement room, placed on the righthand side of the chair/wooden stool. The room has been cleansed of negativity for at least three days prior to the attunement. We have observed the attunement preparation ourselves.

(3) We have meditated and kept a fast as part of preparations.

(4) We have to ask ourselves, now that we are Reiki masters: Are we living by the five principles of Reiki.

(5) What about regression? This is a separate topic by itself. As a Reiki teacher does not teach regression you have to get acquainted with this technique by taking hypnotic therapy classes and ensure that this will include the regression technique.

6) In later chapters in this book we shall discuss some of the problems faced by a Reiki teacher, which please read and understand carefully.

Shall we continue?

5

Problems and Problems

During the courses held by me, most of the time students revert to me with questions. I have been jotting down their questions and the answers given. I sincerely hope these will help you to clear many of your doubts.

The first problem faced by me during the attunements was with one of my students by the name of Pradeep Naik. During the .irst day of attunements all the 12 students were asked of the ex[eriences in the attunement room. Whilst 11 of them talked about their experiences excitedly, only one student was quiet, and he said that there were no experiences.

The problem started on the second day. I took Pradeep in the attunement room and whilst giving him the attunement, he felt dizzy. After the attunements were over, he would not get up. Pradeep has a big build, somehow I picked him up and put him on the bed. I tried to revive him and bring him back to consciousness, but he would not come out of it.

I was scared. What to do? What if he dies? The questions came floating to me. What would you do? Call the doctor? Anyway, I sat in a meditation pose, called for the help of the spiritual guides — Dr. Mikao Usui, Dr. Hayashi, Mrs. Takata and Dr. Pradeep Diwan, my guru, my teacher. I invoked their help. After about a few minutes pictures started floating up on my mental screen and I was pleased.

After coming back to consciousness, I got up and kept my right hand on Pradeep's crown chakra. I visualised a golden light floating to the crown chakra from my right hand and whispered softly, "you are coming back into your body, slowly, I am bringing you back into your body — slow...ly, you are coming back into you body" and I could see Pradeep's eyes started to flicker, I continued with my whispering that he was coming back to his body, and, after a few minutes his eyes were completely opened and he smiled.

While asking for experiences, Pradeep stated when the last attunement was given to him, he felt something come out of his body and his physical self was just left behind.

Pradeep could see himself and me on the bed from the ceiling in the room. He was floating on the ceiling. Pradeep could also hear me very clearly, but did not want to return to the room as he was so happy with this feeling of lightness, this illumination.

The second experience was with Rasik Thakker who just leapt out of his body, and, landed up on the ceiling — floating and seeing himself lying down on the ground. When asked how he felt, he said, "I did not want to come back, it's amazing, unbelievable". This has happened when we did the mind control exercise of "activating your astral body."

Similar experience occurred on "activating your astral body" with Dr. Reshma Gurnani, who sat up, but would not respond to anything being said or instructed to her.

After doing the exercise with her again — special instruction was given: "Now you will return to your body fully, your feet, your calves and your thighs have returned and you feel sensations in these areas. You now feel sensations in your hips, root chakra, sexual chakra, hara and solar plexus. (After a pause) Now, you feel sensations in your chest areas, stomach, shoulders, hands, move your fingers, all the sensations are returning one by one. Your chin, your facial muscles, your forehead all are being activated. Your sensations have now fully returned back to you. Your five senses are working in their perfect condition. Slow...ly open your eyes"

When Dr. Gurnani opened her eyes, we asked her what had happened, and she said that though she could hear everything, she could not open her eyes as they were left out.

There are cases in visual meditation and Reiki that can never end. But, I caution you of one thing — NEVER PANIC! In any situation be calm, if anything goes wrong, please call in your spiritual guides as taught to you in the attunement techniques and request them to help you. Once the spiritual guides come to you they will always help you in every phase of your life.

In visual exercises, though the ethereal body may leave, this has to return to the physical body — it is only a matter of time, just assume that the person has dozed off to sleep. When the person wakes up, he/she will be in excellent/perfect condition.

Even so for Reiki attunement, most of the experiences the students get are seeing of shadows, colours, out of body experiences, geometrical shapes etc. etc.

Remember, during one of the attunements we are opening up the third eye chakra, so these experiences will occur. Nothing to worry about or be scared.

6

What to Do and What not to Do

*Q*uestions, questions and Questions.

How do we know what is wrong with a person?

Answer: On placement of hands over the 26 positions of the body, three minutes per position, if you concentrate, you will come across:

   (i) Cold areas — where you have to do the scooping of bad energy and throw it away in salt water.

  (ii) Areas where too much energy is being absorbed into the patients.

 (iii) Areas where you feel a slight pain in your hands. These areas are the problematic areas.

What to do when I feel and know about the problematic areas?

The first thing is — you never put this to the patient in a blatant way. You can suggest that while giving Reiki you felt some sort of sensations which indicate that there is pain in those area/s. Do you have any problems with that area? Ask innocently. If the patient's answer is negative, suggest that he goes to the doctor and gets a medical check up.

     Remember one thing, Reiki is holistic. We are treating the patient on a mental, physical and spiritual level. The problem may still be prevalent on the auric level and the medical science may not be able to prove what we have proved. The pain may attack the physical body from any time between the day of your giving Reiki upto a six-month period.

7

A Visual Meditation Exercise:
The Balloons and the Stones

- Seat yourself comfortably on a chair with both your feet touching the ground.
- Do the breathing exercise till you feel you have reached the alpha level or feel completely relaxed.
- Visualise someone tying small pebbles on your right hand fingers that are quite heavy.
- Visualise someone tying balloons on your left hand.
- Keep on doing so till you feel heavy on the right hand and light on the left hand.
- Open your eyes.

Results

If you see your right hand is lower than your left hand or your left hand is much higher than your right hand — you can classify that your visualisation is proper.

Continuous practice of this exercise will help you to succeed with tailor-made exercises.

8

Meditation — 20 Minutes

- Sit in any comfortable position you wish to.
- Listen to the sounds around you, the rotating fan, the A/C, birds chirping, people conversing.
- Now, listen to your breathing, in-out, in-out, in-out.
- Next listen to your heart beats.
- Mentally try and count the number of different sounds you can hear.

Next time you sit for this particular meditation exercise try to increase the number of sounds.

9

What if no Results Follow

*O*nce a student asked me, "Mr. Mohan what if we complete the course with you, and no results follow?"

This was my reply to the students: "My class has a maximum of 20 students. If the result is 90 per cent, I consider myself a failure. During each of my class held over a period of two days or approximately 20 hours, special care is taken to follow each student individually, so that no student is left behind. The result is on the second day, at the end of the course, we have a question and answer period, during which an assessment is done on all the students and weak students are pinpointed. These students are requested to come for a refresher course, which is free of charge. Mostly, students do not need to come for more than one refresher course. This ensures that the result is always 100 per cent.

Hence, if the results achieved are always 100 per cent during every training session, the question of "What if NO results follow" does not arise.

During the class session, I never tell the student "we will discuss this later" as it is a known fact that if any question is avoided, there is a chance that the interest of the student may fizzle out. While conversing with any student, eye contact is always maintained. It is a must. That is confidence!

All questions are answered honestly. If the answer is not known, other students are asked to answer that question, if they know the answer.

Students are thus always pleased at the openness and frankness. They know that come whatever may, no wrong teaching will be imparted to them.

Their minds settle down and they feel at ease with themselves and the friendly atmosphere, knowing that whatever they are being taught the teacher knows the subject thoroughly.

10

The Positive and the Negative Mind

*T*here is a very famous saying: "Two men stood behind the bars, one saw mud, the other saw stars"

"Is the glass half full or half empty"? The negative mind will reply "half empty" whilst the positive mind will reply "half full".

The first negative thought that rises in your mind is known as an 'elemental'. This thought is smaller than an atom. The main food for this 'elemental' is your negativity. It feeds on your fears, on your doubts, on your anger, on your failures and on all your minus points.

Then the more you dwell on these, the larger it becomes; the larger it gets, the more difficult it is for you to crush this thought.

Then — all of a sudden — 'BANGGGG' this same elemental crushes you, sending your head spinning around, taking you from the heights of success to the bottom rungs of failure.

Whose fault is it anyway? "Mine," I would say.

Yes — it is your fault if you fail.

Yes — it is your fault if you are unsuccessful.

Yes — it is your fault if you cannot stand up and say, "I am a failure".

Accept things as they are, not as you want them to be. Fight with all the positivity you have in yourself. Customise your visual exercises to change the thoughts in your mind from the darkness of failure and doom to the realms of light and success. Keep on repeating to yourself the most successful phrase ever invented

"Day by day in every way I am getting better and better and better".

See the improvement in yourself. While looking into the mirror each morning do not frown but smile and wish yourself "a very happy good morning".

See yourself flying through the day successfully. Be a positive person, be successful.

11

Why Is a Certificate Necessary?

*T*hat's simple.

How can you differentiate between a fake teacher and a genuine teacher?

The colour of each certificate given is separate.

The Reiki 1 Certificate is blue in colour.

The Reiki 2 Certificate is green in colour.

The Reiki 3A and 3B Certificates are red in colour with a golden label on the left hand side.

No doubt these can be forged. But, ask your sub-conscious mind — have I tried hard to get this certificate?

What's the difference between the genuine teacher and the fake teacher?

Well, the fake teacher will always live in fear of being caught. But, the genuine teacher is never frightened. A genuine teacher is at peace within himself, which over the years reflects in his face, which glows with happiness.

The genuine teacher looks at the certificate with pride and a sense of achievement whilst the fake teacher looks at the certificate with shame, knowing deep within himself that he is a cheat.

Be proud of yourself — work hard at what you want to achieve and feel the difference.

12

Let's Sum Up

*O*nce more we sum up.

We have learnt how to handle the problems. Are you more confident about yourself? No??!! Read Chapter 5 of Reiki 3B again, you are protected by the spiritual guides. Nothing ever will go wrong again, this is the only assurance I can give you.

What goes up comes down. Any student of yours who has an O.B.E. (out of body experience) will have to return to the body. in a matter of time.

Remember also that attunements are given once in a lifetime. Never repeat the attunements again.

Students coming to you fresh will get the attunements from you, whilst students coming to you who have done Reiki from another teacher will not be given attunements for that particular level. So, it is not necessary to charge fees from that student for it will be a refresher course for this student.

If you even have a problem you can write to me via the publisher (e-mail, hot-mail, snail-mail/ postal or can also call me on the phone).

I wish you all the best and pray that you succeed at whatever you do that is positive and good.

13

The Presentation of Certificates

THE JAPANESE TRADITION

*A*fter each course in Reiki is over, the teacher and the students stand in a circle and chant "OM" three times.

After which the teacher calls the name of each student individually. The student comes and stands in front of the teacher.

The teacher bows down from the waist and the student repeats the gesture. The certificate is then presented to the student and they again bow from waist downwards.

This is the usual procedure while presenting the certificate.

14

How to Close Each Day

THE BEAR HUG

*D*uring the end of each session (everyday) the Reiki teacher and the students stand in a round circle, entwine their hands and chant "OM" three times.

After the chanting of the "OM" the Reiki teacher hugs each student individually, whilst all the students hug each other also.

This brings to end the current day's session, only to meet on another day.

15

Questions

*T*he most proper questions to be asked will be on the following lines:

Q. 1: Now that I have completed the full book, can I declare myself as a Reiki master?

Ans: Yes, by completing this course, you are not only a Reiki master, but you are also in a level above the Reiki masters — you are a Reiki teacher — an independent teacher of Reiki. Congratulations.

Q. 2: Can I start my own classes?

Ans: Yes, provided you feel confident yourself. Ask your subconscious mind, "Have I done justice to this course? Have I practised the norms in the book? Do I live with the attitude of gratitude? Have I mastered the symbols? Have I mastered the art of giving Attunements? If your answer to each of the above is "YES", well, go ahead and start your own classes.

Q. 3: When can you visit us?

Ans: It depends on my itinerary. You will be given ample notice to be free during that time. The date/time will be advised to you on your e-mail or by fax. If you delay or are late due to whatsoever the reasons — the appointment will be cancelled.

Q. 4: Will you be giving us attunements for all the three levels during you visit?

Ans: No, the certificates issued to you were assessed on your experiences while you received the attunements from your partner. If they were fictitious, it is your doing. But, if they were genuine,

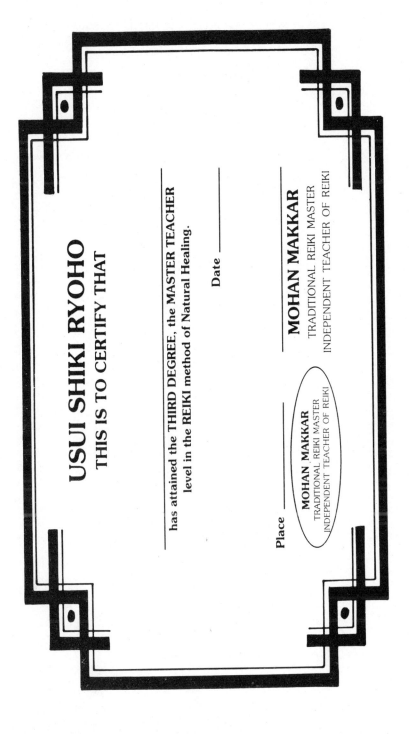

USUI SHIKI RYOHO

THIS IS TO CERTIFY THAT

has attained the THIRD DEGREE, the MASTER TEACHER
level in the REIKI method of Natural Healing.

Date _____

Place _____

MOHAN MAKKAR
TRADITIONAL REIKI MASTER
INDEPENDENT TEACHER OF REIKI

MOHAN MAKKAR
TRADITIONAL REIKI MASTER
INDEPENDENT TEACHER OF REIKI

you do not need another attunement. These are only given once in a lifespan.

Q. 5: What if we want only the attunements?

Ans: Sorry, this cannot be done. You have to attend a proper course that is conducted on regular basis.

Q. 6: What if we want to attend your course?

Ans: Please write to me on my e-mail or hotmail address and we shall revert. My regular class fees are:

Reiki Course 1 — US$25 — 2 days' course from 9.00 a.m. to 5.00 p.m. each day

Reiki Course 2 — US$50 — 2½ days' course

Reiki Masters 3A — US$100 — 5 hours' course. It is must for students to attend and practice Reiki 1 and 2 courses on repeated regular course to get a hang of the full course and Reiki positions plus should be in a position to answer questions posited by the students.

Q. 7: What is your itinerary?

Ans: Depends on response of each territory.

Q. 8: Now that I have purchased this book, what should I do?

Ans: This book is unique. Every book in the market has a serial No. Here is what you do.

(a) Tear off the perforated first page — fill it up and post it to us. Ensure all sections are completely filled.

(b) After each Reiki degree is complete, we can provide you with a Reiki Certificate subject to your answers being satisfactory. Else, we give you two additional chances, after which your card will be deleted.

(c) If all the answers are right, the certificate will be posted to you within 45 days.

(d) You will automatically be advised of my visit to your territory. If you wish to have the master/teachers certificate please let us know in advance.

Look out for: Going for publication shortly

The Healing Angels

Another Book by

Mohan Makkar

It was all so sudden.

Lina called me and said "Mr. Mohan, this girl keeps on coming in my dream every night — can you tell me who she is or what she wants?"

"Are you frightened Lina?" I asked.

"No," she replied.

"Then why do you want to know who she is?" I queried.

"I want to know," she insisted.

"Okay — close your eyes and visualise her in front of you". I gave in and instructed her. (At this stage I did not know what I was doing or getting at — just my sixth sense started leading me).

She just "Hmmm'd" me.

"Mentally call her in front of you".

Again "Hmmm".

"Ask her name".

A puse and then.

"Maria," she whispered softly to me.

"Ask Maria why she has come to you?"

Again, a pause, then.

"Hmmm".

"Lina, request her to become your everlasting, permanent friend".

A pause, then.

"Hmmm".

"Thank her for coming to you".

"Hmmm".

"Take a few deep breaths and open your eyes".

A l-o-n-g pause and then:

"Thank you Mr. Mohan — who is this Maria" asked Lina.

"MARIA is your HEALING ANGEL — Lina".

"What?" she shrieked in excitement.

Yes, it was the first time it happened to Lina, next was Usha, then Meena, Manoj, Gautam and like dominoes — all the students attending the meditation classes got their Angels. Now, these Healing Angels are healing people on physical/mental & spiritual levels. The more the students meditate the stronger the Angels become.

Seeing this miracle, I thought WHY NOT? If 18 of my students can get this power — WHY NOT THE WORLD?

So, here it is to you — WORLD — An Angel for every Soul on this Earth.

May the Golden Healing Light shine on you with every breath you take.

Mohan Makkar